EARLY
AMERICAN
PHILOSOPHERS

EARLY
AMERICAN
PHILOSOPHERS

ADAM LEROY JONES

FREDERICK UNGAR PUBLISHING CO.
NEW YORK

First printed 1898

Reissued 1958

Printed in the United States of America

Library of Congress Catalog Card No. 58-9336

CONTENTS

INTRODUCTION

A HISTORICAL view of the progress of philosophical thought in America reveals little that can be classed as distinctively American. The general attention of the people has turned to what is practical, meaning by that word, whatever tends to promote the welfare of society as well as that of the individual. Such an attitude is inevitable in a young and growing people. The nation, like the individual, must pass through a period of material and mental growth and development before it can make a worthy effort to explain to itself the meaning of its environment and of its own life and activity. It must develop the power of thinking and acquire a knowledge of the world before it can attempt to solve the problems and discover the fundamental principles of that world. Activity is the characteristic of this early period; contemplation comes only at maturity. But as the individual may be influenced, even early in life, by the thought of maturer minds, so may that body of individuals, known as the race, be influenced by the philosophy of older civilizations, long before a philosophy of its own is possible.

Thus we find that the thought of America has been strongly influenced by all the great schools of European thought: more recently by the English and Post-Kantian systems; earlier in the century by the Scottish Common Sense School; in the Colonial Period by Locke and Berkeley. Besides these wider influences, almost every thinker of importance has been listened to. We may note as one of the characteristics of our people, the readiness with which it has received and made use of whatever seemed to be of worth in any and every system. In the effort to attain a broad culture it has neglected no available means. This is especially manifest in the attention that has from the first been given to the problem of education; schools and libraries have been universal; the aims and methods of education have received an ever-increasing attention.

The department of philosophy that has awakened most interest is that branch which gives expression to the practical tendency already alluded to, and which is also closely allied to educational interests, viz.: Ethics.

The earliest of our writers considered it most important, and the works which have been written upon it during the present century are very numerous. Most of these have no great importance, but the fact that they were written is evidence of the place which the subject occupied in the thought of the people.

Our present task is not, however, to attempt to determine the characteristics of American thought or to enter minutely into its history. Only a short period will be considered; that which preceded the War for Independence. The prevailing influence was the philosophy of Locke, and to some extent that of Berkeley. We should not expect to find an independent philosophy; the people were English, and the philosophy which we find is naturally a development of the English philosophy of that time. We can not even call this a movement of the people as a whole. The clergy alone had the education and the taste for speculative inquiries, and very few of the clergy had any sympathy for such study. The two foremost thinkers, Jonathan Edwards and Samuel Johnson, were idealists of the Berkeleyan type, but this idealism can not be regarded as a logical outcome of Puritanism. These men were led to their conclusions by working out the philosophy which they had received, the one from Locke, the other from Berkeley. Their philosophy was not an outgrowth of the theology which they were taught. The Puritan tendency was better represented by the view that condemned Philosophy

and Ethics as contrary to religion. Johnson adhered to
the ideal system and made it a part of all his thought, but
he had early abandoned the Puritan creed and the Puritan
attitude. Edwards worked out his idealism early in life[1] before he was wholly dominated by the received dogmas. He
never formally renounced this philosophy, and some passages
in his later works seem to indicate that he still accepted it, but
it plays a very small part in his maturer thought.

For a short time in the middle of the eighteenth century,
idealism was received with favor in Princeton College; but the
inauguration of John Witherspoon, who introduced the Scot-
ish Philosophy of Common Sense, was the signal for the
abandonment of Berkeleyanism.[2] The newer school seemed
to give the best expression to the Neo-Platonic dualism of the
Puritan doctrines. For a long time, the Scottish Philosophy was
very widely received. The ethics of the early Americans was
influenced chiefly by the contemporary English and Scotch
Ethics. The Cambridge Platonists, the Esthetic and Moral
Sense Schools, and the doctrines of Malebranche and his
follower Norris, were all influential in varying degrees.

[1] There has been some disagreement as to the time when Edwards wrote his
Notes, in which his idealism is found. The question has been conclusively decided by Professor Egbert C. Smyth, who has examined the original manuscripts.
V. *Some Early Writings of Jonathan Edwards. Proceedings of the American
Antiquarian Society*, October 23, 1895. It has been urged that Edwards was
indebted to Berkeley. He never mentions Berkeley's name; the points in which
he differs from Berkeley are more numerous than those in which he agrees, if we
except what both received from Locke; and the evidence brought forward to
prove such indebtedness has been insufficient. The question does not, however,
concern the main purpose of the present essay.

[2] V. McCosh, *Scottish Philosophy*. The best literature on this period is found
in chapters ix–x of George Lyon's *L'Idealisme en Angleterre*, Paris, 1888.

CHAPTER I

I. WILLIAM BRATTLE, 1662–1717

Before taking up the philosophy of Edwards and Johnson, we shall consider briefly several names of lesser importance in this connection, but yet well worthy of some attention.

William Brattle[1] is the first whom we shall notice here. His claim rests on his authorship of a text-book in logic—the first on that subject by any American.[2] He was born in Boston in the year 1662, graduated from Harvard College eighteen years later and was tutor there from 1686 to 1696. The rest of his life was spent as a clergyman in Cambridge. As a tutor he was a great favorite with the students, and received from them the title of " Father of the College." As a minister he opposed the narrowing theology then predominant, and represented in many ways a more humanitarian attitude.

The full title of his book was *Compendium Logicæ Secundum Principia D. Renati Cartesii Plerumque Efformatum et Catechistice Propositum.* It is hard to determine the date at which this work first appeared. It seems to have been printed for the first time in 1734. The author died in 1717. It is known that it was long used as a text-book in its manuscript form. It must have been written before 1717, and it seems probable that it may have appeared during the time that Brattle was a tutor *i. e.*, prior to 1696. As the title indicates, it is founded on the principles of Descartes. The text bears no marks of Locke's influence, but the notes which were added in the printed editions (1734, 1753) abound in references to the English philosophy. Locke's essay on the Human Understanding was published in 1690. In a community so entirely English, and so closely in touch with the English Puritans as was that of Boston, the influence of the Puritan Locke must have penetrated very early, and if Locke had been known to the author of the *Compendium Logicæ* we should surely see traces of his influence in that work. Furthermore, it seems more reasonable to suppose that a text-book should have been written at the time when its author was engaged in the work of teaching such subjects rather than during his subsequent life as a minister. But however this may be, the work in question undoubtedly has the merit of being the first work of an American on the subject of logic.

In the printed form and including the notes it occupies only sixty octavo pages. It is written entirely in Latin, and is put in the form of question and answer. The Prolegomena contains the definitions of terms, the principles of the division of Logic and the rules of certitude. The main work is divided into four parts, three of them corresponding to the mental processes of preception, jndgment and reasoning, and the fourth treating of method.

Logic is defined as the art of thinking, or the art of the use of our reason in comparative cognition. The operations of the mind are given as four, apprehension, judgment, reasoning and construction (*compositio*). The use of Logic is like that of a medicine to the body; it aids in freeing the mind from the defects of ignorance and forgetfulness, doubt and error, confusion, obscurity and the like. The rules of certainty given are first, nothing is to be admitted as true so long as it includes anything of doubt; second, we should beware of trusting too much to the senses; third, what we perceive we perceive by the mind alone; and fourth, that is true which we know clearly and distinctly.

Part I deals with ideas and the simple contemplation of things which are considered under the heads of modes of perception, objects of perception, primary and secondary, and relations. It includes a scholastic discussion of substance, affections and the various relations of perceptions.

Part II is concerned with judgment and considers the various kinds of propositions.

Part III has to do with reasoning and discusses argumentation and the syllogism.

Finally, part IV is a brief consideration of method.[3]

This book had a long period of usefulness and was used as a text-book in Harvard College until 1765.

2. BENJAMIN FRANKLIN, 1706–1790

Benjamin Franklin's[1] direct contribution to philosophy was small. Preëminent in politics and practical affairs, he thought metaphysics little worthy of attention, as he believed there was no practical benefit to be derived from such study.. He arrived at this conclusion very early in life and with one exception he always adhered to it. He read *Locke's Essay on the Human Understanding* and the *Port Royal Logic* in his sixteenth year (1722) and it was the reading of these which convinced him of the futility of philosophy. At about the same time he read Shaftesbury and Collins, and these writings strengthened him in his attitude of doubt toward many of the accepted beliefs. It was probably from Collins also that he drew most of his arguments for his one essay in Metaphysics. The title of this essay is *A Dissertation on Liberty and Necessity, Pleasure and Pain.*[2] It was occasioned by the reading of Wollaston's *Religion of Nature Deliniated.* Franklin was in England at this time (1725), and had met with this book while working as a printer in London. He afterwards considered the publication of the Dissertation an error, and most of the edition was destroyed. It is short, occupying only thirty-two octavo pages. He takes as the motto the verses from Dryden beginning " whatever is, is in its nature just, since all things are by Fate." He concludes from the goodness, wisdom and power of God that nothing can be wrong in the world and that there is no real distinction between vice and virtue. His argument is as follows:

" There is said to be a first mover who is called God, the maker of the universe; He is said to be all-wise, all-good, all-powerful." These propositions he conceives to be generally admitted, and on them he bases his argument.

" If He is all-good, whatsoever He doeth must be good.

" If He is all wise, whatsoever He doeth must be wise." These he belives to be self-evident and undeniable if the first two propositions are admitted.

" If He is all-powerful there can be nothing either existing or acting under the universe against or without His will; and what He consents to must be good because He is good; therefore evil doth not exist." To admit the existence of evil, Franklin says, is contrary either to the all-goodness of God or to his all-powerfulness. For there is nothing in the universe but what God does or permits. If He permits evil, it must be from lack of power or inclination to hinder it. To say that God permits evil that good may come is an argument that destroys itself, for whatever an infinitely good God hath wise ends in suffering to be, must be good, is thereby made good and cannot be otherwise.

" If a creature is made by God it must depend upon God and receive all its power from Him; with which power the creature can do nothing contrary to the will of God, because God is almighty; what is not contrary to His will must be agreeable to it, must be good because He is good; therefore a creature can do nothing but what is good." The act which is called evil cannot be so; neither can the pain or punishments which follow such acts be an evil. Mr. Wollaston argues that every action done according to truth is good, every action contrary to truth is evil. But when a man commits a theft he acts according to a truth, i. e, his inclination to steal.

" If the creature is thus limited in his actions, being able to do only such things as God would have him do and not being able to refuse doing what God would have done, then he can have no such thing as free-will or power to do or to refrain an

action." Liberty is sometimes understood to mean absence of
opposition; but this liberty is like that which an object has to
fall to the ground; it is at the same time necessitated to fall,
it has no freedom to remain suspended. Suppose man were a
free agent. He is part of the great machine of the universe,
and his regular acting is requisite to the regular moving of the
whole. There are before him many objects of choice of which
only one is the right one. To know which is right and best
he would need to know all the consequences of each. Only
omniscience could know this. As man cannot know this he
can only chance to hit the right one. If the right one is not
done, the harmony of the whole is disturbed. Can we suppose
Providence would take less care of the moral than of the
natural system, which is ruled by invariable laws?

" If there is no such thing as free will in creatures there can
be neither merit nor demerit in creatures."

" And therefore every creature must be equally esteemed by
the Creator."

" To sum up the argument : When the Creator first designed
the universe either it was His will and intention that all things
should exist and be in the manner they are at this time, or it
was His will they should be otherwise, *i. e.*, in a different manner. To say it was His will things should be otherwise than
they are, is to say somewhat hath contradicted His will and
broken His measures, which is impossible, because inconsistent with His power. Therefore, we must allow that all things
exist now in a manner agreeable to His will, and in consequence of that are all equally good and therefore equally
esteemed by Him."

In the second part of his Dissertation, Franklin discusses
pleasure and pain. He asserts that pain is caused by something outside the mind, and that it is pain that first awakens
consciousness. Pain or uneasiness is the first spring and cause
of all action ; if all uneasiness, or what is the same thing, all desire, should cease, there would be no longer any voluntary

motion anywhere in the universe. The fact that all actions are caused by the desire to be free from uneasiness, or in other words, by self-love, is a further proof that there is neither merit nor demerit.

" This desire is always fulfilled or satisfied," either by the attainment of its object or by the removal of the desire. The last uneasiness or pain is removed by the sweet sleep of death.

" The fulfilling or satisfaction of this desire produces the sensation of pleasure, great or small, in exact proportion to the desire." Pleasures are caused by the accomplishment of our desires, desires are caused by pain; hence pleasure is caused by pain. Therefore the sensation of pleasure is equal or in exact proportion to pain. This being true, the argument for a future life from the predominance of pain is not sound.

All the Creator's works are equally used by Him, and no condition of life or being is in itself better or preferable to another, nor is life preferable to insensibility. The ancients supposed an elysium or a state where all was pleasure without pain. From the nature of pleasure and pain such a state would be impossible. Pleasure would soon pall upon us without pain.

" The immateriality of the soul is made an argument for immortality. . . . Though the soul may be immaterial, we know that consciousness, which is its action, may cease. All our ideas are first admitted by the senses and imprinted on the brain; there they become subjects of the soul's action. . . . The soul is a mere power of contemplating on and comparing those ideas when it has them; thence springs reason. But the soul must have ideas before it can think." To remember a thing is to have the idea of it still plainly imprinted on the brain, which the soul can turn to and contemplate on occasion. When we have lost the ideas of anything we can think no more upon it. At death the body is destroyed and the ideas of the brain are likewise necessarily destroyed, and the soul, though incapable of destruction, must cease to think or act, leaving nothing to act upon. To cease to think is little different from ceasing to be. "It is not impossible that the same faculty of contemplating ideas may hereafter be united to another body and receive a new set of ideas, but that will no way concern us who are now living, for the identity will be lost; it will no longer be the same self but a new being."

Franklin's Psychology and Logic are certainly crude and full of errors. Still it is probable that there was much of that sort of thinking in the century that followed Locke. Franklin himself was dissatisfied with this, as he was later with his deism. His conclusion is interesting. He decided that his reasonings might be right but were not useful, so he abandoned them. That is the conclusion on which most of his countrymen have acted in regard to such questions ever since his time.

Franklin's aid in the advancement of education was of much greater importance. He established a public library in Philadelphia; he organized the "Junto" for the discussion of topics of interest and for mutual improvement; he established the Philosophical Society for the discussion of scientific questions, and it was his energy, tact and perseverance that made possible the Academy which grew into the University of Pennsylvania.

Franklin's views on education are to be found in his *Proposals Relating to the Education of Youth in Pennsylvania.*[1] He had read the works of Locke, Milton and others on this subject, and knew whereof he spoke. He mentions first the value of education as the surest foundation of the happiness both of the family and of the commonwealth, and urges the need which exists in the colonies for better facilities for education. In his plan for an academy he recommends that the situation be healthful and pleasant; that the building be furnished with a library, with maps and globes, mathematical instruments, apparatus for experiments in science, prints of all kinds, prospects, buildings and machines. He recommends a plain diet and an abundance of exercise.

As it is impossible for the pupils to study everything that is useful and everything that is ornamental, they should be taught what is most useful and most ornamental. First of all he mentions penmanship, drawing and mathematics. The best English writers are proposed as the materials for the study of the mother-tongue, and care in reading and the cultivation of a clear style are insisted upon. Geography, chronology and ancient customs can be taught with advantage in connection with the reading of history; this reading is especially useful in teaching morality, religion and good citizenship, as well as logic and reasoning. Natural history and the history of commerce and invention are also very useful. Different languages should be taught according to the intended profession of the student.

Franklin was especially favorable to the establishment of an English school, but the advocates of a Latin school were greatly in the majority; an attempt was made to carry on an English school also, but it met with little success. The most noticeable feature of his views on education are his appreciation and recommendation of physical training and the study of history, and the high place he gives to the study of English language and literature.

Franklin's practical and humanitarian attitude has been regarded as representative of the spirit of the American people. There is much reason for this opinion.

3. CADWALLADER COLDEN, 1688–1776

Cadwallader Colden should find a place among scientists rather than among philosophers. His work in botany was especially valuable. But his interest in philosophical questions and one of his essays give him some title to a place among philosophers. He was born and educated in Scotland, but came to America early in life. He was prominent in political affairs in the colony of New York and was deeply interested in scientific questions. In a correspondence[1] with Samuel Johnson he criticises Berkeley's idealism, but his criticisms do not merit particular mention.   In 1745, he published an essay entitled *An Explication of the First Cause of Action in Matter and of the Cause of Gravitation.*   Chapter I treats of the primary material agents or the first principles in physics. Matter he defines as that which is extended and impenetrable. These are the essential properties of all matter, but there may be different kinds of matter.   The first of these is the power of resistance.   He conceives of resistance as an active force differing from the other two kinds of matter, which are moving force and elastic or expansive force.   Resistance is negative to both these.   He enters into a discussion on the nature of resistance and of elasticity, but we cannot follow him here. His conclusion is, matter is really power, action or force: action without motion is not inconceivable; thinking, he says, is an example of such action.   It was probably his conception of matter as some force, something active, that prevented his comprehension of Johnson's identification of action and intelligence.

His second chapter is on the cause of gravitation; he explains it by the pressure of the ether on the two bodies.   The pressure is in proportion to the depth of the ether which is pressing upon a body.   The depth is less between one body and another than it is on their opposite sides; hence the pressure on the sides nearest each other is least.   Therefore the greater pressure from the opposite sides pushes them together.

4. THOMAS CLAP, 1703–1767

Thomas Clap,[1] President of Yale College, published, in 1765, *An Essay on the Nature and Foundation of Virtue and Moral Obligation.*   The author was born in 1703 and died in 1767. He graduated from Harvard College in 1722.   After preaching for a number of years he was made rector of Yale College in 1740.   During his presidency he did much to improve the state of the college in promoting the study of science, improving the library and revising the laws for the government of the institution. His work on Ethics appeared near the close of his life. It was written as a text-book—*A short introduction to the study of Ethics for the use of students.*

He states in the preface his purpose, which is to discover the foundation of moral obligation; this he believed had not been done in the many books of rules that had appeared. He professes to follow in general Norris's *Ideal World.* Four subjects are proposed for consideration: the nature and standard of moral virtues; the obligation to conform to that standard; how the knowledge of the standard is to be gained; and finally a scheme of moral duties and virtues.

Moral virtue is defined as conformity to the moral perfections of God. We get our ideas of these perfections from the small degrees of them which we see in creatures; these extended to an infinite degree give us our idea of God's perfection. The perfection of creatures is in their resemblance to God. His perfection is in His being what He is. The divine perfections are either natural, as eternity, omniscience etc., or moral, as holiness, justice, goodness and truth.

God, when He makes a creature, communicates to him some degree of His own perfection. If the creature has reason and can perceive the moral relations of things, he is a moral agent and is capable of moral virtue and obligation—moral obligation. Moral virtue is conformity to the moral perfections of God. This conformity may be internal or real, depending on a moral temper or disposition of the mind which is like to God; or external or apparent, proceeding from some lower motive.

Obligation to conform to the moral perfection of God arises from three things.

First, from the infinite and absolute perfection of the divine nature. He is the only perfect, self-existent being, and He must be the only rule and pattern for His creatures, who derive their perfection from Him. The perfection of the rational creature is to continue in the perfection wherein he was created.

The second basis of moral obligation is the declared will and law of God.

This is increased by the third, which is the sovereign power and authority of God. Rewards and punishments do not create obligations, but they are subordinate motives and incentives to act according to it.

Following this is a discussion of the other theories which have proposed other ends of conduct. The theory which makes self-love the one end and aim is an absolute inversion of the order, dignity and perfection of beings. "It makes a small part bigger than the whole."

Benevolence is a good principle, but is only one of the perfections which every moral agent ought to have.

Moral sense or taste so far as it exists in the mind of a mere natural and unenlightened man may proceed wholly from self-love. It is not the same as conscience, which is a judgment of actions as agreeable or disagreeable to the law of God. If taste were the rule there would be as many rules as there are vitiated tastes among mankind.

Reason is insufficient as the basis of moral obligation. The term is vague, and even if rightly understood it must have some data or principle to act on. As a power it can not be an original standard of action. It can not be so excellent as to be the criterion of divine favor or to claim supreme authority; this would make man his own lawgiver. It is too general to be the special criterion of moral virtue.

Moral fitness is too vague a term to serve as a criterion of virtue.

Conformity to truth is a true principle if truth means the perfections of God; if it means the truth of fact it can not determine moral action.

Right and wrong are also too vague. To set up right as the standard is to set up a thing which is not God as a standard for God. If this were the criterion there would be many and various ideas of right.

Obedience to the will and command of God in order to promote one's own happiness is the principle of self-interest. All these principles may be admitted if kept subordinate to the main principle.

The author believes that divine revelation alone can show us how to know what the perfections of God are and what disposition and conduct in us are a conformity to those perfections. His scheme of moral duties and virtues requires no especial notice. Crude and poor as this essay is, it serves to show that there was a demand for a scientific foundation of the principles of conduct. This was the third work on Ethics that had appeared in America after 1740, the other two being those of Edwards and Johnson.

1. WILLIAM BRATTLE

[1] Josiah Quincy, *History of Harvard University*, passim.

[2] Charles Morton's manuscript logic was used in Harvard College before that of Brattle appeared. He brought manuscript text-books to America which he had used in his private school in England; *Massachusetts Historical Society Collections*, vol. ii, p. 115.

[3] Brattle's work is similar to the *Port Royal Logic*, which he may have seen.

2. BENJAMIN FRANKLIN

[1] For Life and Education of Franklin v. *Autobiography*.

[2] Parton's *Life of Franklin*, vol. i, app. ii.

[3] Jared Sparks' *Works of Franklin*, vol. i, chap. viii, ix, app. iii.

3. CADWALLADER COLDEN

[1] Beardsley, *Life of Samuel Johnson*.

4. THOMAS CLAP

[1] V. especially Dexter, *Yale Biographies and Annals*.

CHAPTER II

1. *Life and Education*

SAMUEL JOHNSON has many claims to careful consideration in any review of philosophy in America. He was the earliest and the most prominent exponent of Berkeley's system outside of England; he saw even further than Berkeley, and caught a glimpse of the truths that receive their development at the hands of another and a greater school of thought. Johnson was the first American to formulate a system of ethics; he was one of the first to give to education that thought and attention which his countrymen have continued to devote to it. His biography was first written by the Rev. T. B. Chandler in 1805. Later and more complete is the *Life and Correspondence of Samuel Johnson* by Rev. E. E. Beardsley (New York, 1874). These and his unpublished autobiography[1] are the chief sources of information as to the events of his life.

He was born in Guilford, Conn., in 1696. He made rapid progress in his youthful studies and his parents resolved to send him to the new college at Saybrook (the beginning of Yale College). He entered that institution at the age of fourteen. The course then given was far from thorough. It included the study of Cicero and Virgil, the reading of the New Testament in Greek, the merest rudiments of science, a smattering of scholastic philosophy and a considerable training in Calvinistic theology. During Johnson's course, Descartes, Locke and Newton began to be heard of,[2] but students were cautioned against reading them, as it was feared that they might be inimical to the existing theological doctrines; it was not until

22   [370

Johnson himself was a tutor in the college that their writings were introduced. The library consisted chiefly of books that had been brought from the mother country sixty or seventy years before.

But Johnson was an earnest student; he was especially proficient in linguistic studies, and was the chief orator of the college.[3] It was customary at that time for the students to make synopses of the books which were accessible, and Johnson showed an unusual aptitude for this work of abridgment and classification. He had mastered almost all that was to be gained in this way when he chanced to come upon a copy of Bacon's *Instauratio Magna*. This work "opened to him a new world of thought;" "he found himself like one at once emerging out of the glimmer of twilight into the full light of open day." His mind was thus prepared for the reception of new ideas; it was a turning point in his mental career.

After leaving college, he taught for a time in his native town; a little later he was appointed tutor in the college. In 1720 he became a Congregational minister. After several years of doubt and hesitation, he felt it his duty to leave that church and enter the Church of England. This step required courage and independence. The Puritanic theology was predominant, almost universal; Johnson's family and friends opposed the change; it would be necessary to make a long and dangerous journey to England for orders. But he persevered in his resolves; in 1722 he sailed from Boston to return a year later as missionary to the town of Stratford. Here he passed more than thirty years of his life. It was during this period that Berkeley spent two years in America awaiting in vain the establishment of the college in Bermuda. He received several visits from Johnson and they carried on a considerable correspondence, relating principally to Berkeley's philosophical system. Johnson had already adopted it as a whole, but he had many questions to ask and some objections to propose for discussion. These letters are among the sources to which we must go for Johnson's thought. When Berkeley returned to England, he was easily induced by his friend to interest himself in the college at New Haven, and the gift of his library and estate was of great value for the advancement of education.

Johnson's interest in education had not ended with his college course. He prepared many students for college, and he was respected as an authority in educational matters throughout the colonies. Benjamin Franklin consulted him in the organization of the Academy at Philadelphia and urged him to accept the presidency of the institution. Johnson readily gave his advice and assistance, but could not persuade himself to leave his parochial duties. At about the same time a project was matured for founding a college in New York; his services were again required; the trustees finally assured him that the success of the undertaking depended upon him alone, and he at last consented to become its head. In 1754 he removed to New York and began his duties in the new capacity.

When he retired from the presidency nine years later he left the college well-established, after conducting it successfully through one of the most trying periods of its existence. Dr. Johnson died in Stratford in 1772. As a scholar he was perhaps unsurpassed by any American of his time. He was not only acquainted with theological and philosophical writings, he was also interested in science and literature. He received the degree of Master of Arts from both Cambridge and Oxford Universities and later the degree of Doctor of Divinity also from the latter.

In his thinking he was careful and independent. He came to new questions with an openness of mind and a candor that was remarkable at a time when prejudice was unusually predominant. His philosophy is to be found in his text-books on Logic and Ethics and in his correspondence. In 1723 he published an *Introduction to the Study of Philosophy* exhibiting a general view of the arts and sciences. In 1746, under the pseudonym Aristocles, he published in Boston *A System of*

Morality, a work on Ethics. While his sons were in college he wrote for their assistance a *Manual of Logic and Metaphysics*. This with the *System of Morality* was afterwards published under the title of *Elementa Philosophica* (Benjamin Franklin pub. Phila. 1752: 2nd ed. London 1754.) It was used as a text-book in the college at Philadelphia, and probably in Johnson's classes in King's College also.

In 1767 he published a *Hebrew and English Grammar*[4] (2nd ed. 1775). The second edition of this work contains his synopsis or classification of knowledge.

We have already seen how the reading of Bacon had broadened Johnson's mind. He was in consequence more ready to give new views a careful examination, and this attitude made it easy for him to accept Berkeley's philosophical system. It is hard to determine when he first met with Berkeley's works. He had many opportunities to hear of them through his correspondence with theological friends in England; especially as Berkeley was prominent in church circles. He had at any rate read the new philosophy before Berkeley's arrival in America. It had recommended itself to him at once. He believed that the contradictions which the system seemed to present to the common view, were only apparent. Moreover his interest in religion made him favorable to the ideal theory, as he thought he found in it the strongest defence against scepticism. It is true that he criticised it in some of its details, as appears from his correspondence with Berkeley, and these objections must have had some weight, since Berkeley begs him to remember that these works were written while their author was very young, and that defects are on that account to be expected; he then briefly explains and defends his theory; in a later letter he speaks especially of archetypes, of space, of time and of abstract ideas, which seem to have been questions on which they did not wholly agree. But Berkeley did not urge his views in minor points. He was content that the main doctrine should be accepted. Johnson not only accepted it but gave it a concrete expression; he presented it in a form less obnoxious to the common view, and avoided ambiguities in Berkeley's statements which the latter had inherited from Locke; and he made some important developments and applications of this doctrine.

2. *Psychology*

In his psychology Johnson departs somewhat from his predecessors, but his position is similar to theirs in many respects. In regard to innate ideas we find the following: " Our minds may be said to be created mere tabula rasa. They have no ' notices' of any kind properly created in them or concreated with them."[5] By this explicit statement, he excluded all ready-made ideas and notions from the mind and avoided the confusion attaching to Locke's denial of innate ideas: yet he left himself free to ascribe to the mind certain inherent activities and principles of activity.

He continues:[6] " The ' notices' which the mind has, derive originally from (or rather by means of) the two fountains of sense and consciousness. By means of the senses we receive simple ideas. These are sorted out into a vast variety of fixed combinations or compound ideas distinct from each other, in which the simple ideas are always found to co-exist; of these compounded ideas consists every individual body in nature, such as we call horse, tree, etc. These various distinct combinations, connected together in such a manner as to constitute one most beautiful and harmonious whole, make up what we call universal nature or the entire sensible or natural world. In the reception of these ideas or objects of sense, we find that our minds are passive, it not being in our power (supposing our organs rightly disposed and situated) whether we will see light and colors, hear sounds, etc, or not."

" By consciousness[7] is meant our perception of objects *ab intra*, or from reflecting or turning the eye of the mind inward and observing what passes within itself, whereby we know that we perceive sensible objects and their connections, all the pleasures and pains attending them and all the powers and faculties of our minds employed about them."

" I find moreover that when I have had any perception or impression of sense, I retain a faint image of it in my mind afterwards. This power of the mind is called imagination or memory, which implies a conciousness of the original impression. Memory may imply recollection of intellectual as well as sense-given objects. We are also conscious of a power whereby we can not only imagine things as being what they really are, but can also join such parts and properties of things together as never co-existed in nature ; these must be also referred to the imagination, but as influenced by the will."[8] " But besides the powers of sense and imagination,[9] we are conscious of what is called pure intellect, or the power of conceiving (abstracted or) spiritual objects and the relation between our several ideas and conceptions, exertions and actions of our minds, and the complex notions resulting from all these. These cannot properly be called ideas, they being entirely of a different kind from the objects of sense and imagination."

" The word ' idea ' [10] as commonly used by modern writers signifies any immediate object of the mind in thinking, whether sensible or intellectual, and so in effect is synonymous with thought, which comprehends both. For a more distinct understanding of ourselves it may be best to confine the word idea to the immediate objects of sense and imagination and to use the word notion or conception to signify the objects of consciousness and pure intellect."

Locke was chiefly responsible for this confusion in the use of the word idea. Berkeley, in his later writings, suggests a distinction between idea and notion, but he never draws the line so definitely as we find it here. Johnson continues, " As ideas combined and connected make up the sensible world, so notions or conceptions and what relates to them make up the entire spiritual or moral world."

The powers of the pure intellect[11] are (1) simple apprehension of objects and their relations; (2) judging of true or false according as things appear to agree or disagree, to be connected or not connected one with another; (3) reasoning or inferring one thing from another, and methodizing things according to their connections and order; (4) affecting or disaffecting things as they appear good or bad, agreeable or disagreeable to us, i. e. attended with pleasure or uneasiness; (5) willing or nilling, choosing or refusing according as we affect or disaffect them, with liberty of acting or forbearing to act in consequence of the judgment we have made of them.

This classification of the powers of the intellect is a further attempt at a more scientific analysis of consciousness. The distinction of the pure intellect from sensation was of primary importance, and these distinctions and analyses constitute a real contribution to the psychology of the eighteenth century. He did not, it is true, separate clearly the productive and the reproductive imagination. He saw that the will was influential in the former, but he assigned no distinct and separate terms to the two processes.

These were developments from the psychology which he had received from Berkeley; we come now to a doctrine wherein he leaves Berkeley's guidance and adopts a principle which was not furnished by empirical psychology. He does not propose innate ideas or principles in the sense in which they were understood by Locke; he does not assert that we can have knowledge without experience; but experience once given, there are certain truths of intuition as certainly known as are those of sensation. In short there are for him, certain *synthetic a priori propositions*,[12] though he does not call them by that name. We shall see how he believed them to be possible. This is his statement;[13] " No sooner does any object strike the senses or is received in our imagination or apprehended by our understanding but we are immediately conscious of a kind of intellectual light within us (if

I may so call it), whereby we not only know that we perceive
the object but directly apply ourselves to the consideration of
it both in itself, its properties and powers and as it stands related to all other things, and we find that we are enabled by
this intellectual light to perceive these objects and their relations in like manner as by sensible light we are enabled to
perceive the objects of sense and their various situations ; so
our minds are passive in this intellectual light as they are to
sensible light and can no more withstand the evidence of
it than they can withstand the evidence of sense. Thus I
am under the same necessity to assent to this —that I am
or have a being and that I perceive and freely exert myself,
as I am of assenting to this—that I see colors or hear
sounds. I am as perfectly sure that $2 + 2 = 4$, or that the
whole is equal to all its parts, as that I feel heat or cold, or that
I see the sun. I am intuitively certain of both. This intellectual light I conceive of, as if it were a medium of knowledge just as sensible light is of sight. In both these is the
power of perceiving and the object perceived ; and this is the
medium by which I am enabled to know it. This light is also
one common to all intelligent beings. By it, all at once see
things to be true or right, in all places at the same time, and
alike invariably at all time, past, present and to come. If it be
asked, whence does this light derive whereby all created minds
at once perceive as by a common standard the same thing to
be true and right, I answer, I have no other way to conceive
how I come to be affected with this intuitive intellectual light
whereof I am conscious, than by deriving it from the universal
presence and action of Deity. For I know I am not the author of it myself, being passive and not active with regard to
it, though I am active in consequence of it. Therefore though
I cannot explain the manner how I am impressed with it (as
neither can I how I am impressed with objects of sense), I
humbly conceive that God does as truly and immediately en-
lighten my mind internally to know these intellectual objects

as he does by the light of the sun enable me to perceive sensible objects.

"And this intuitive knowledge, as far as it goes, must be the first principles from which the mind takes its rise, and upon which it proceeds in all its subsequent improvements and reasonings." "I conceive it is from this intuitive intellectual light that we derive taste and judgment, and with respect to morals, what some call moral sense or conscience." Such is his method of explaining these intuitive principles. He thought that he found warrant for this use of intellectual light in Plato,[14] and he was undoubtedly influenced by the Cambridge Platonists also. His familiarity with the sensationalistic psychology led him to seek an explanation of the perception of these facts in something analogous to sense-perception. And this intellectual light was for him the explanation of moral principles as well. The most important fact is his recognition of the intuitive principles thus known. Mathematical propositions, for instance, are here as with Kant universal and necessary for all rational beings, or, as he states it, for all created minds. Locke and Berkeley had not denied these from Johnson's point of view; they had not taken his point of view. What Locke opposed was the belief that these ideas could be in the mind without experience. Whether they could be innate in another sense was a question which he did not try to answer.

The mind being endowed with this intellectual light, and the powers before mentioned, advances as follows in the acquisition of knowledge:[15] "As soon as the mind is possessed of any variety of objects, being assisted by the inward intellectual light, it immediately falls to contemplating its ideas and conceptions and to comparing them with one another. And here the first thing it is enlightened to know is its own existence from the existence of its perceptions, exertions and their objects, which it conceives as real beings or things, and hence gets its notion of being in general. But even this first object of knowledge it is made to know from that first principle of intellectual light, flowing from the parent mind, namely, that perception, action and being perceived or acted upon, imply existence; for the truth of this principle or proposition the mind has an inward, an intuitive sense and certainty. Hence, it immediately infers, I perceive and act, therefore I am. I perceive such an object, therefore it is."

Johnson has here added to Descartes' first principle; not *I perceive*, but *I perceive and act*, therefore I am; and this brings us to another doctrine in which Johnson did much original thinking—a doctrine which is a central principle in modern educational theories; it owes its present importance to the German philosophy and especially to Hegel—the doctrine of self-activity.

Locke and Berkeley had admitted that the mind is active, but they were more interested in the operations wherein it is passive, especially in perception, and although some activity is not denied, it receives little attention. Johnson emphasized the activity.

" Mind or spirit," he says,[16] " signifies any intelligent self-active being. We take this notion from what we are conscious of in ourselves. We know that each of us is a conscious perceptive, active and self-exerting being." His conception of the self-activity of the mind is inseparable from his doctrine of cause, and can be better understood after considering the latter.

3. *Cause and Mind*

" By the word cause[17] we mean that being by whose design and activity, force or exertion another being exists; that being which exists by the design, force, action or exertion of another is called an effect; what is called an effect must be supposed not to have existed and consequently to have had a beginning of existence or at least a dependent existence, and must therefore have had a cause by the force or activity of which it came into existence and without which it would not have been; this, therefore, must be the case of everything that is, till you come to a first cause, *i. e.* to a being that never had a beginning or any dependent existence—a being that exists by the absolute necessity of his own nature, having an original perfect fullness of being in and of himself without dependency on any other. Such a being there must be, otherwise nothing could ever have been unless you can suppose a thing to be its own cause, *i. e.* to act before it is, which is impossible; or unless you suppose an infinite succession of causes and effects, which, in effect, would be an infinite effect without any cause at all. But an effect without a cause is a contradiction in terms; for by the definition, to everything that is produced there must be a correspondent power adequate to the production of it or an active force sufficient to produce it. There are indeed many things that occur to the senses and thoughts that appear at first sight to be agents or causes, which, strictly speaking, are not so, as we find upon a more careful scrutiny, though they are vulgarly called so. So we say, the sun warms, enlivens, ripens the fruits; whereas we find upon a more strict enquiry that it is by no means the adequate cause; the sun and (what we call) other natural causes, are in themselves passive inert beings connected with one another according to the established laws of nature; so that, being things merely passive and inert, they cannot, properly speaking, be the causes of the effects vulgarly ascribed to them; they must therefore be called only signs, occasions, means or instruments, and we must look for some other being in whom resides, and by whom must be exerted, that adequate power or force by which the effect is truly produced which, therefore, is the true and real cause; as the others can only be called the apparent causes, having no real efficiency or activity in the production of the effect."

" Certain activities of our bodies take place without any design or activity of ours. These may be called, with regard to us, necessary effects. On the other hand, we walk, speak,

write, etc., from a principle of conscious, designed self-exertion
or voluntary activity; these, therefore, are called free or
voluntary effects with regard to us, which we produce or not
as we please: in doing which we are voluntary causes, and
produce voluntary effects. By voluntary effects we mean such
as are produced by a free voluntary cause acting from a principle of self-exertion, exciting a force of its own or from within
itself, which it chooses to exert and might do otherwise. This
is properly called a cause, an efficient cause or agent; whence
it appears that only intelligent active beings or spirits can be
truly efficient causes, which alone are properly called causes."

This conception of cause was foreign to the English philosophy of the time, and marks another important advance. Consciousness, intelligence or self-active cause is for him the only
real cause. His defence of this doctrine is found in his correspondence with Lieut. Gov. Colden, of New York. The
latter writes:[18] " I am desirous to be more fully informed how
consciousness and intelligence become essential to all agents
that act from a power in themselves." Johnson answers:[19]
" A power of action without a principle of self-exertion and
activity, I can form no notion of. . . . As it is not the part of
a philosopher to multiply beings and causes without necessity,
it seems plain to me that we ought not to imagine any other
principle of action than the principle of intelligence which we
know from our own soul in fact has and in nature must have
a power of self-exertion and activity." At another time he
says:[20] " When we speak of matter and the action of it, we
use that word for want of a better, in a sense rather figurative
than literal, and understand it in a vulgar sense rather than in
a sense that is strictly philosophical [as we] do the rising and
setting of the sun. So we may call writing the action of the
pen when it is really merely acted, and consequently that by
the action of matter you do not mean any exertion of its own,
much less a designed, conscious self-exertion, which always
enters into my notion of efficient causes, and that, therefore,

when you say it is determined by the exertion of efficient
causes always external to itself, those efficient causes must
always be self-exerting and intelligent beings, *i. e.*, spirits,
which, therefore, only are properly agents, and consequently
that all the actions in all nature that affect our senses, and excite ideas in our minds, are really the action of the Great
Supreme Being or Spirit."

The question was again raised when Colden received Johnson's *Elementa Philosophica.*[21]   He writes: "You say our perceptions cannot be produced in our minds without a cause (so
far we agree), or, which is the same thing, by any imagined,
unintelligent, inert or unactive cause. I likewise agree that
an unactive cause and no cause are synonymous, but I am not
convinced that intelligence is an essential concomitant to all
action, for then I could not conceive the action of a mill without supposing it endowed with intelligence."

In reply, Johnson repeats the law of parsimony as his principal reason for denying the existence of any principle of
action other than intelligence, " *Non est philosophia extera mul-
tiplicare sine necessitate:* and a blind principle or power of
action seems repugnant and useless. You allow that the
action of what you call matter is, according to you, derived
from and directed by the Intelligent Being. And so matter is
no more than merely his instrument, so that what you call the
action of a mill or watch is really only a successive series of
passions till you come to the principle of intelligence, which
will ultimately prove to be also the principle of the action."

Thus, in his conception of cause as well as of mind Johnson
was in advance of his century. The definition of mind given
by an able American thinker [22] of the present century well ex-
presses Johnson's view: "Mind is a creative first cause," and
for him a cause which is not a creative self-active cause is not
a cause at all.

I. SAMUEL JOHNSON'S LIFE AND EDUCATION.

[1] I am indebted to The Ven. Archd. Geo. D. Johnson for access to a copy of the manuscript autobiography.

[2] *Autobiography.* [3] Dexter, *Yale College Annals*, vol. i, p. 115.

[4] This contains also his classification of knowledge.

[5] *Elements of Philosophy, Noetica*, ch. i, 5.

[6] *Ibid.*, 5, 6, 7. [7] *Ibid.*, 11.

[8] *Cf. Berkeley's Introduction* (10) *to Principles of Human Knowledge, De Motu*, 53.

[9] *Noetica*, ch. i, 12. *Cf. Berkeley's Works*, Ed. Fraser, vol. i, p. 285.

[10] Ch. i, 4. He discusses in this connection Plato's use of the term.

[11] Ch. i, 12. [12] *Cf.* Kant. [13] Ch. i, 13, 14.

[14] *Republic*, vi. "When the soul has fastened on an object over which real truth and real existence are shining, it seizes that object by an act of reason." He refers also to Fenelon, Norris, Malbranche and Cudworth.

[15] *Noetica*, ch. ii, 2. [16] Ch. i, 2. [17] Ch. ii, 4–7.

[18] Letter of June 2, 1746, *Beardsley's Life of Johnson.*

[19] June 19, 1746. [20] April 15, 1747. [21] December 20, 1752.

[22] R. G. Hazard.

CHAPTER III

SAMUEL JOHNSON—CONTINUED

1. *External Reality*

His conception of EXTERNAL REALITY[1] is like that of Berkeley. " The ideas or objects of sense are commonly supposed to be pictures or representations of things without us, and indeed external to any mind, even to that of the Deity himself ; and the truth or reality of them is conceived to consist in their being exact pictures of things or objects without us, which are supposed to be the real things ; but it is impossible for us to conceive what is without our minds, and consequently what those supposed originals are, and whether these ideas of ours are just resemblances of them or not. I am, therefore, apt to think that these ideas or immediate objects of sense are the real things, at least all we are concerned with, I mean of the sensible kind ; and that the reality of them consists in their stability and consistency, or their being, in a stable manner, exhibited to our minds or produced in them, and in a steady connection with each other, conformable to certain fixed laws of nature, which the great Father of Spirits hath established to himself, according to which he constantly operates and affects our minds. Thus, for instance, there is a fixed, stable connection between things tangible and things visible, or the immediate objects of touch and sight, depending, as I conceive, immediately upon the permanent will and fiat of the Creator. By this, however, it is not meant that visible objects are pictures of tangible objects (which is all the sense that can be made of our ideas of sense being images of real things without us), for they are entirely different and distinct

36   [384

things, as different as the sound triangle and the figure signified by it. All that can be meant by it is, that as tangible
things are the things immediately capable of producing (or
rather being attended with) sensible pleasure and pain in us
. . . so the immediate objects of sight, or visible things, are
always, by the same stable law of our nature, connected with
them as signs of them and ever correspondent and proportioned
to them." " I know external objects because I perceive them;
not that their existence depends on my mind, but on that
mind by which I am enabled to perceive them."

" It is not to be doubted that there are archetypes of these
sensible ideas existing external to our minds, but then they
must exist in some other mind and be ideas also as well as
ours; because an idea can resemble nothing but an idea; and
an idea ever implies, in the very nature of it, relation to a mind
in which it exists. But then those archetypes or originals
and the manner of their existence in the eternal mind must be
entirely different from that of their existence in our minds.
In him they must exist as in original intellect, in us by way of
sense and imagination; in him as originals, in us only as faint
copies."

The chapters of the *Elementa Philosophica* which deal with
formal logic require no extended comment. They present a
clear and concise formulation of deductive logic as it was
commonly received in the eighteenth century.

2. Ethics

Johnson divided knowledge [2] into science, the knowledge of
truth considered speculatively, and art, the knowledge of truth
considered as directive of practice. This division is regarded
as valid at the present time. Learning may be divided into
(1) Philology or the study of words, which includes grammar,
rhetoric, oratory, history, geography, poetry and criticism;
and (2) Philosophy, or the study of things, including logic, the
mental sciences, theology and ethics, which includes moral

philosophy, economics and politics. In his *Elementa Philosophica* the first part or *Noetica* dealt principally with logic and metaphysics. The ethics or second part, deals with moral philosophy. In his treatment of this subject Johnson formulates a system which is apparently founded on utilitarian principles, but he not only avoids a conflict with religion, but really makes it the most important part of his doctrine. Furthermore he reconciles the conflicting ethical theories of the day and brings them all under his central principle. His ethical theory may be considered a Theological Utilitarianism.[3] It anticipates Paleys and is like it in many respects. The germs of such a theory are to be found in Berkeley's writings, but Berkeley never developed a complete ethical theory. His nearest approach to it was made in his *Discourse on Passive Obedience*.[4]

Johnson defines moral philosophy [5] as "the knowledge of the moral world, the world of spirit or free intelligent agents, and the general laws of the moral behavior, together with all that practical conduct thereon depending that is necessary to promote our true happiness, both in our present and future state." In other words, "Ethics is the art of living happily by the right knowledge of ourselves and the practice of virtue; our happiness being the end and virtue the means to that end." We are said to live happily when we enjoy ourselves and all that is really good for us in the whole of our nature and duration, *i. e.*, considered not only as sensitive, but as reasonable, free, active, social and immortal creatures. For happiness means that pleasure which arises in us from enjoyment of ourselves and all that is really good for us or suitable to our natures, and conducive to our well being in the whole. It depends on a good habit or state of the soul united with and delighting in its proper objects, which are truth and good; the first being the object of the understanding and the other of the will and affections, and this good habit is the same thing with virtue. Virtue consists in that integrity, firmness and stability of soul

whereby we honestly and steadfastly persist, in spite of all
temptations to the contrary, in the love and practice of moral
good and the hatred and forbearance of moral evil. Vice is the
contrary of this. Moral good consists in freely choosing and
doing whatsoever truth and right reason dictate as necessary
to be chosen and done, in order to our own true moral happiness. For moral good must mean the good of a moral agent,
that is of a rational conscious, free, self-exerting and self-
determining agent."

Two things must be considered in respect to moral good:
the criterion of right conduct and the obligation to practice it.
The criterion of an action is its natural good or the pleasure
or happiness in the whole of our nature and duration which
naturally attends it. For we find by experience that some
actions are, by their nature, attended with pleasure or happiness and some are attended with pain or misery. Ease, pleasure or happiness is what we call a natural good. But in order
to make a natural good the test of the moral we must take
into account the whole of our nature and duration, as being
sensitive and rational, social and immortal creatures. It must,
therefore, be the good and happiness of the whole human
nature and the whole moral system in time and to all eternity.
Hence, the good of the animal body in pleasure of sense is but
imaginary, and ceases to be good and hath even the nature of
evil, so far as it is inconsistent with the good and happiness of
the soul. This is also the case with private good so far as it
is inconsistent with the good of the public; and temporal good
so far as it is inconsistent with that which is eternal. Now this
good and happiness in the whole coincides with and even re-
sults from the truth and nature of things. The general good
of the whole, the nature and fitness of things and the truth of
things really coincide in settling the criterion of right and
wrong. We may say then that "moral good must consist in
freely choosing and acting conformably to the nature of things,
which is again the same as acting according to right reason,

since it is by right reason that we apprehend things as they really are and the effects they tend to produce."

"The obligation to practice virtue implies a law binding us to such action as morally good, and to forbear the contrary. This constitutes the notion of sin and duty and is two-fold, natural and internal, or external and moral." The natural and internal obligation arises from a law of our nature implanted by the Creator. It includes (1) the law of reason and conscience, which is the same as the moral sense; (2) the law of self-love and self-preservation arising from consciousness of self and of pleasure and pain; (3) the law of benevolence; the self and social good can not be considered as at all interfering, but as being entirely coincident and subservient to each other. Action in accordance with these principles would be what is commonly called virtue or vice, but there would be nothing in it of religion, which must ever enter into a just and complete notion of morality. Morality requires also the external and moral obligation. It includes, first, the political obligation to conform our actions to the welfare of the family and the public; and second, the religious obligation, or the consideration that the actions which tend to our happiness in the whole, are the will and law of God enforced by the sanctions of eternal rewards and punishments. For he being perfectly happy and self-sufficient to his own happiness cannot aim at any advantage to himself in giving us being, or in any of his dispensations towards us, and consequently that his end must be our happiness.

Thus morality in its whole extent is the same thing with the religion of nature, or that religion which is founded in the nature of things. Concluding then that truth and duty are thus necessarily connected, the author announces as the purpose of his essay, the search of the truths that relate to ourselves, to our fellow-creatures and to God; and after finding the truths to deduce the duties. The first task is the problem of the "speculative part" of his moral philosophy, and the second is that of the "practical part."

Part I, chapter I, considers the nature of man, his excel-
lencies and imperfections.   Chapter II has for its subject,
"The Author of our nature, His perfections and operations."
He gives three proofs of the existence of God: that from the
existence of ourselves as imperfect beings we must conclude
that there is a perfect creator; that the existence of a necessarily eternal being is proved by the existence of necessary
and eternal truth; and that the order and design exhibited in
the universe necessarily presuppose an infinite intelligent cause.
Chapter III considers the end of man's creation and the future
state.   It includes a proof of immortality.   He argues from
the fact that we have an earnest aspiration for eternal life, that
God must certainly have provided an object suitable and correspondent to the noble aspiration which he has created in the
mind of man.[6]   He asserts that it is no objection to the pos-
sibility of immortality to say that it is inconceivable; for so
have many things been in our experience until they came to
pass.

Part II or the practical part of moral philosophy deals with
the various duties which we owe to ourselves, to one another,
and to God, and closes with a discussion of the connection between the law or religion of nature and Christianity, followed
by a philosophical prayer.

It is not our purpose here to point out the weak places in
this system of ethics.   It has certainly some merits: it is the
first work on this subject produced in America; it is free from
the bias of any theological school, and it reconciles, in some
degree, what is best in the English ethical theories of that time.

3. *Samuel Johnson as an Educator.*

We have already mentioned in the sketch of Johnson's life
some of his practical services to education.   He had been a
teacher before graduating from college.   At twenty years of
age he was a tutor in Yale.   During his life as a minister he
prepared many students for college.   His advice was valued

by Franklin and many others.   He made King's College possible.   His published 'works were written in the interest of
education and were used at the University of Pennsylvania and
doubtless at King's College also.

His educational theory so far as it is formulated is in the Preface, Introduction and the sixth chapter of the *Noetica*.   In
this preface he gives, as his reason for publishing the work,
the usefulness of such manuals of science to beginners.   They
make it possible for the student to " at once behold, as it
were, in miniature, the objects, boundaries, ends and uses of
each of the sciences ; their foundation in the nature of things,
the natural order wherein they lie and their several relations
and connections."   " As in the natural world one cannot have
a just notion of any particular country without considering its
situation in relation to the whole globe nor of any particular
globe without considering its situation in relation to the
whole system ; so in the intellectual world neither can we
have a just notion of any particular science wthout considering it as it stands related to the whole circle of learning and
the general end pursued through the whole.   Such a short
draft may also be of use to students to direct and methodize
their thoughts."   He here recognizes an important pedagogical principle which is valid to-day.

His conception of the progress of the mind in knowledge is
as follows :[7] " The first notices of the mind are doubtless those
of sense, but directly joined with a consciousness of its perception.   And every fresh notice of sense and consciousness
tends to excite its admiration and gain its attention. . . .
Thus by degrees, having a great number of feelings, tastes,
odors, sounds and visible objects, frequently repeating their
several impressions, and its conscious memory still enlarging,
it begins, by means of the intellectual light, gradually to
collect and recollect the several relations and connections it
observes to obtain among its various ideas.   Distance, situation, the connection of things tangible with things visible,

etc., must be learned by experience, as well as the names of things and the connection and use of words, also the use of the limbs, the organs of speech, etc. All these things require a great deal of application, and the exercise of much thought and exertion. So that it seems evident that these little creatures (children) from the beginning do consider, reflect and think much more than we commonly imagine. The reason why so many little, low, weak and childish things appear in them, which we are apt to despise and think beneath our notice, is not for want of good sense and capacity, but merely for want of experience and opportunity for intellectual improvement. Hence also it appears that we ought to think little children to be persons of much more importance than we usually apprehend them to be; and how indulgent we should be to their inquisitive curiosity, as being strangers; with how much candor, patience and care we ought to bear with them, and instruct them; with how much decency, honor and integrity we ought to treat them; and how careful it concerns us to be, not to say or do anything to them or before them that savors of falsehood or deceit, or that is in any kind indecent or vicious. *Pueris maxima debetur reverentia* is a good trite old saying." This respect for childhood is one of the strongest notes in Johnson's educational doctrine. It seems very remarkable to find such a principle so clearly expressed at a time when Jonathan Edwards could publicly assert that children were "like little vipers." The prominence which Johnson gave to this humanitarian principle did not grow out of the Puritan attitude toward life, but was, we believe, an original contribution from the man himself.

As to the development of the child-mind, he continues: "While children are acquiring a general knowledge of the sensible world about them, they are at the same time acquiring a notion of *meum* and *tuum*, and thence a quick sense of justice: and soon they come to acquire the notions of free agency, of praise and blame, the notions of law and conscience.

The great concern of culture and right education is to awaken their attention to the inward intuitive sense of true and false, good and bad, right and wrong. They should be continually encouraged and assisted, for being in a world where everything is new and strange, they are liable to many mistakes in their apprehensions, and to blunders in their actions and conduct, and yet in their original simplicity and well-meaning are ordinarily very willing to be taught and conducted. They should be taught to control their appetites and passions, to value the good-will of their fellows, and to gain it by kind and honest actions, and to recognize their connection with the community, kingdom and all mankind, and a conduct corresponding to the whole of these duties.

" In the meantime they should be taught to read and write, and their minds should be improved by reading understandingly the most interesting and engaging things in history, poetry, morality, and especially the Holy Scriptures.

"Care should be taken and means contrived, as far as can consist with good government, to put and keep them always in a good humor, which will make everything take the better effect."

This principle is another in which Johnson was in advance of his age ; that study should be made a pleasure did not occur to many teachers of that century, and it would have met with little favor from most of them.

Education should then proceed by teaching music and numbers, but these mnst not consist of mere abstractions, but be turned as much as possible to facts and things practical and useful in life. By the time they are ten or twelve years old they may be taught from maps a general notion of the earth, the situations of the several countries and kingdoms upon it, with some sketch of the history of the several nations inhabiting it, and at the same time, from schemes and globes, a considerable notion of the heavens and the system of the world in general, as well as the globe of the earth in particular. They should be initiated into grammar and language by the time they are six or seven years old. At the same time the connection between their own and other languages should be explained by instructing them in English, Latin and French grammar, and a few years later in Greek and Hebrew. By the time they are sixteen or eighteen, they should have studied also Rhetoric, Poetry, Mythology, as well as History and Chronology. They should then take up Metaphysics and Logic, Higher Mathematics, the Fine Arts. They should have studied Natural History and the Natural Sciences, and finally Moral Philosophy, Ethics and Theology, besides Economics and Politics. We may sum up Johnson's chief pedagogical principles as follows: proceed from the general to the particular; from the concrete to the abstract; respect the personality of the child; make his work pleasant for him if possible, and give primary emphasis to the development of the moral side of the character.

[1] *Noetica*, ch. i, 8–10.

[2] *Elements of Philosophy*, Introduction.

[3] *Berkeley's Works*, edited by Fraser, vol. iii, p. 110, note.

[4] *Ibid.*, vol. iii, p. 106 *et seq.*

[5] *Elements of Philosophy*, Ethica, Introduction.

[6] *Cf. Berkeley; Guardian* No. 27, April 11, 1713.

[7] *Noetica*, ch. vi, and Introduction.

CHAPTER IV

1. *Life and Education*

JONATHAN EDWARDS[1] was born in East Windsor, Conn., in the year 1703. His father was a Puritan minister, and a man of unusual scholarship for that period. His maternal grandfather was likewise a Puritan minister of some note. His mother is described as a woman of remarkable judgment, prudence and piety, and superior to her husband in native vigor of understanding. We are told that she had received a good education.

It was the intellectual power and independence of the mother rather than the scholarly tastes of the father that reappear in the son.

Jonathan was the only son in a family of eleven children. He received his early education at the hands of his father and elder sisters. As a child he was sensitive and affectionate and very precocious. Being the only son of a Puritan minister in a thoroughly Puritan community, his attention was early turned to questions of religion and theology. At the age of eleven years he wrote a letter refuting the idea of the materiality of the soul.[2] This letter is worthy of mention as showing the bent of his youthful mind; both in its method and its aim, it foreshadows his later work. Its aim is the defence of his religious beliefs; its method of argument is his favorite *reductio ad absurdum.*

At about the same time he wrote a letter to one of his father's correspondents minutely describing the habits of the "American Spider."[3] His description shows that he was an

46   [394

acute observer, and although some of his conclusions were erroneous, most of them have been confirmed. His interest in nature was later overshadowed by theology, but his passion for speculation was a characteristic which continued with him through life.

He entered Yale College in his thirteenth year, graduating four years later with the highest honors. During his second year in college he read Locke's essay on the Human Understanding, and his interest was at once turned to philosophy. He recorded his own views and his difficulties in his *Notes on Mind.*⁴ This was to be an extensive work; its intended scope is indicated in the sub-title, *The Natural History of the Mental World or of the Internal World*, being a Particular Enquiry into the Nature of the Human Mind with respect to both its Faculties, the Understanding and the Will, and its various Instincts and active and passive Powers. These notes, though only fragments, contain a system of philosophy and the germs of most of Edwards' later philosophical principles.

Besides the *Notes on Mind* there is a series of *Notes on Natural Sciences*,⁵ which were likewise intended to form the basis of a comprehensive work. He recorded observations and conclusions in Astronomy, Meteorology, Geology, Atomic Theory, etc., so remarkable that an able scientist⁶ has asserted that "if Edwards had devoted himself to physical science he might have added another Newton to the extraordinary age in which he commenced his career."

But Edwards' theological interest was not dormant during this period, for he was writing at about the same time his *Notes on the Scriptures* and his *Miscellanies*, both of which dealt chiefly with religious topics. Very soon these questions came to occupy all his thought. Some of the prevailing dogmas of the Puritan creed were distasteful, even repulsive to him. Still he did not question their validity, and he finally after many struggles reconciled himself to them. This period of storm and stress was concluded in the five years following his graduation from college, and its record is written in his *Resolutions* and his *Religious Diary*. Succeeding at last in quieting his objections to the theology of his fathers, he thereafter devoted himself chiefly to the defense and propagation of these doctrines. He spent a short time as minister in New York. In 1724 he was a tutor in Yale College, where he performed his duties with ability and dignity. In 1726 he was chosen colleague to his grandfather, the Rev. Solomon Stoddard, pastor of the church in Northampton. For a time he was very successful, but as he grew older the ascetic element in his nature gradually became predominant. He was an earnest and powerful preacher, but his increasing emphasis on the most rigid and unsympathetic elements in his theology seemed to neutralize the influence of his naturally affectionate nature. Difficulties arose between himself and his congregation, and he received his dismissal after twenty-four years of service. During this time he had written his *Treatise on the Religious Affections* and various theological works, besides many sermons which were widely read.

In 1751 he removed to Stockbridge, Mass., as missionary to the Indians. Six years later he was called to the presidency of the College of New Jersey. His death occurred March 22, 1758, only two months after he had taken his seat.

He had published the *Enquiry into the Freedom of the Will*, in 1754; it was followed in the next year by the *Treatise on the Nature of True Virtue* and *God's End in the Creation of the World*. These works, with the *Religious Affections*, the *Notes on Mind* and *Natural Science*, and the posthumously published *Lectures on Charity and its Fruits* contain his philosophical and ethical thought. It must be remembered that Edwards' opportunity for gaining a knowledge of philosophical writings was very limited. The course of study then given in the American Colleges was very elementary, and the philosophy studied was mainly that of the scholastic theologians. The study of Greek was mostly confined to the New

Testament; contemporary English philosophy was frowned upon. Locke was admitted at about the time that Edwards entered college, and he was the starting point of Edwards' thought. Edwards was perhaps influenced to some extent by Cudworth's writings, some of which he seems to have read,[7] and he would find in them a summary of Greek philosophy. However that may be, Locke was the strongest influence and to Locke he continually refers.

The style of his writing is obscure and heavy in the extreme. He aimed only at the exact expression of his thought and seems to have made no effort to attain clearness. His lifelong habit of writing down his thoughts as they occurred to him, and his other habit of pursuing any line of thought to its end, no doubt aided him in thinking, but his isolation and his lack of experience in the oral discussion of philosophical questions prevented his realization of the necessity of clear statement. In some of his sermons he rises almost to eloquence, and there his sentences are well constructed and full of energy, but this is true of none of his philosophical works.

2. Psychology

Edwards' psychology takes its starting point in Locke, but a logical carrying out of some of Locke's doctrines convinced him that many of those positions were untenable. He seems at first to follow his teacher in regard to the origin of ideas: "All ideas begin from sensation, and there can never be any idea, thought or act of the mind unless the mind first received some ideas from sensation or some other way equivalent, wherein the mind is wholly passive in receiving them." [8]

The mind is passive in perception, which is " the mere presence of an idea in the mind." He would agree with Locke that there are no innate ideas in the sense of ready-made images or concepts, but he conceives that in some respects thoughts and judgments may be innate.[9] Yet he never works out the problem, nor does he tell us in what respect ideas may

be innate. In a discussion on reason and cause, he gives a
hint of what his answer might be. He announces as an innate
principle " that natural, unavoidable, invariable disposition of
the mind, when it sees a thing begin to be, to conclude certainly
that there is a cause." [10]   " This is an innate principle in the
sense that the soul is born with it—a necessary fatal propensity so to conclude on every occasion." If there are no innate
ideas, he concludes that there is at least one innate principle.

In regard to simple and complex ideas and modes of ideas,
he follows Locke's use without comment or criticism.[11]   The
process by which we arrive at abstract ideas does receive some
attention. " It is not merely a tying of them (ideas) under the
same name, for I do believe that deaf and dumb persons abstract and distribute things into kinds. But it is so putting
them together that the mind resolves hereafter to think of them
together, under a common notion, as if they were a collective
substance . . . for it has abstracted that which belongs alike
to all." [12]

Edwards, like Johnson, had seen the confusion arising from
the use of the term idea to cover all the immediate objects of
the mind or all " subjective thoughts," [13] but he does not sug-
gest any limitation of its meaning and continues to use the
term without qualification.

" Consciousness is the mind's perceiving what is in itself,
ideas, actions, passions and everything that is there percept-
ible: it is a sort of feeling within itself." [14]   The problem of
defining consciousness was one of those which presented itself
to Edwards very early, but it was also one in which he failed
to arrive at a satisfactory solution.

Perception, as we saw above, is merely having ideas. An
act of " judgment, or assent to a thing as true or dissent from
it as false, differs from perception, and so is not the perception
of the agreement and disagreement of ideas."[15]   How it differs
from perception and what it really is, we are nowhere clearly
told. His other expressions on this subject add little light.

There is an act of judgment in memory—a judgment that the remembered ideas were formerly in the mind,[16] *i. e.*, recognition. He implies that men may not be entirely to blame for their judgments and beliefs.[17] Hence, he did not consider judgment wholly an action of the mind in the sense in which will is an action. There may, he believes, be erroneous judgments, but sensations (perceptions) are not in ordinary circumstances fallible in anything. The mistakes of judgment are due to lack of experience.[18]

" Reasoning differs from perception and memory only in the power of having voluntary actions about one's thoughts. It is an act of will in bringing its ideas into contemplation, and ranging and comparing them in reflection and abstraction."[19] We can only conclude from these statements that he believed judgment and reasoning to possess some of the characteristics of both perception and will.

"Knowledge is not the perception of the agreement and disagreement of ideas, but rather the perception of the union or disunion of ideas or the perceiving whether two or more ideas belong to one another. Perhaps it cannot properly be said that we see the agreement of ideas unless we see how they agree. But we may see that they are united and know that they belong to one another, though we do not know how they are tied together."[20]

"Memory is the identity in some degree of ideas that we formerly had in our minds with a consciousness that we formerly had them, and a supposition that their former being in the mind is the cause of their being in us at present. There is not only the presence of the same ideas that were in our minds formerly but also an act of judgment that they were there formerly, and that judgment not properly from proof, but from natural necessity arising from a law of nature."[21]

The acts so far considered would be included under the understanding, which is the speculative part of the mind. The only other mental faculty which Edwards ascribes to the mind is that of the will.   This includes emotions, desires, volitions, in short everything that is not included under the acts of the understanding.   He defines will as "the prevailing inclination of the mind with regard to its own immediate actions;[22] the love of happiness and the capacity of enjoying and suffering are identified with it.[23]   Affections and passions are only strong exercises of the will.[24]   In the *Freedom of the Will*, will is defined as "that by which the mind chooses anything; the faculty of the will is that power or principle of the mind by which it is capable of choosing; an act of will is an act of choice." Imperfect analysis is one of the greatest faults of Edwards' reasoning; it is especially noticeable in his work on the *Freedom of the Will*.

But the most striking development in Edwards' psychology is his formulation of the doctrine of the Association of Ideas.   Here again Locke's Essay was the point of departure.   It was before the time of Hume, and Edwards did not know the earlier writings on the subject.   Hence he lacked the opportunities that Hume had to derive suggestions from sources other than Locke.   In the Essay on the Human Understanding the association of ideas was invoked to account for the unusual connections of ideas.   A natural connection of ideas was taken for granted and was not analyzed.   Edwards uses the term "connection of ideas" to express the general law, and reserves "association of ideas" for a special use. His statement is as follows: "Concerning the laws by which ideas follow each other or call up one another, in which one thing comes into the mind after another in the course of our thinking.   How far this is owing to the association of ideas and how far to any relation of cause and effect or any other relation, and whether the whole may not be reduced to these following: (1) Association of Ideas; (2) Resemblance of some kind; (3) and that natural disposition in us, when we see anything begin to be, to suppose it to be owing to a cause."[25]   His use of the laws of Resemblance and Cause and Effect corresponds

to that of Hume. Those connections not covered by these
two laws are put by Hume under the law of Contiguity in
time and space, by Edwards they are put under the special
law of " Association ;" Hume used the latter term to designate
the general law. The difference between them is a matter of
terminology. It is true that Edwards' presentation of the
doctrine is tentative and was never completely developed, but
so far as it is developed it is equal to Hume's doctrine. He
fully realized the value of these principles. " If it were not for
this mutual attraction of ideas, how rarely our minds would
serve us ; how the mind would be without ideas except as
suggested by the senses."[26] Reasoning and contemplation
depend upon it ; it serves further in the explanation of the appetites which, he says, " consist in some present pain attended
with the idea of ease habitually connected with the idea of a
certain object." " A longing for a particular thing comes
from an idea of pleasure or of the removal of pain associated
with that object.[27] Words come by custom to have certain
associations, and thus influence our thoughts and actions.[28]
Many prejudices arise in this way.[29] The training of animals
is possible only by virtue of the association of ideas."[30] This
is Edwards' contribution to the doctrine of Association and
although it had no influence in the development of the doctrine it does indicate the independence and originality of his
thinking.

Some of the other psychological problems that interested
Edwards may be noticed here. As to the union of mind and
body, he says : " The mind is so united with the body that an
alteration is caused in the body by every action of the mind."[31]
" The common conception of mind is very gross. Mind cannot be said to be in the place where the body is, except in the
sense that all created spirits have clearer and more strongly
impressed ideas of things, and can produce effects in the place
where the body is. In the same sense the mind may be said
to be in the brain."[32] Edwards' development of idealism per-

mitted him to make a more satisfactory explanation of the union of mind and body. The question of personal identity also attracted his attention. He at first agreed with Locke that it consisted in identity of consciousness.[33] But he afterwards considered this explanation insufficient. He conceived it possible that a being might be annihilated and another being created with the same ideas in his mind that the former being had and with like apprehension that he had them before, and yet be in no way connected with the first being.[34] He concludes that identity has never yet been explained.[35]

It is interesting to note that he identifies all men with the first man as a justification for his theological doctrine of *Imputation*.[36] Identity in this case seems to mean continuity, as it does in his *Notes on Natural Science* where he says, "All things that grow are nothing but branches of the first tree, and the seeds from which our trees proceed are no new plants, but branches of the old, a continuation of the first plant in its infinite regular progress."[37]

Many other questions are raised both in the *Notes on Mind* and in those on *Natural Science*, but those already mentioned serve to show Edwards' general attitude in psychology; those that are cited hereafter bear more directly on his philosophical doctrine.

[1] *Biographies* by S. E. Dwight, A. V. G. Allen, Hopkins and Miller. The edition of the works used is that of S. E. Dwight.

[2] *Works*, vol. i, p. 20.   [3] *Ibid.*, p. 23.

[4] *Ibid.*, pp. 664–702.   [5] *Ibid.*, pp. 702–761.

[6] Benjamin Silliman, *American Journal of Sciences and Arts*, vol. xxi, p. 109 *et seq.*

[7] He quotes in the *Notes on Mind*, Cudworth's paraphrase of Plato's description of the "Subterranean Cave."

[8] *Notes on Mind, Series* i, No. 27.   [9] *Ibid.*, i, 52.

[10] *Ibid., Series* ii, 54, p. 689, vol. i, of the *Works*.

[11] *Ibid.*, ii, 41, 42, p. 684.

[12] *Ibid.*, ii, 7, p. 683. No reference is made to Berkeley's doctrine of abstract

ideas. This could hardly have been the case if he had known Berkeley's philosophy.

[13] *Ibid.*, i. 51.   [14] *Ibid.*, ii, 16.   [15] *Ibid.*, i, 28.

[16] *Ibid.*, ii, 69, p. 680.   [17] *Ibid.*, i, 18.   [18] *Ibid.*. ii, 53, p. 687.

[19] *Ibid.*, ii, 59, p. 682.   [20] *Ibid.*, ii, 71, p. 690.   [21] *Ibid.*, ii, 69, p. 680.

[22] *Ibid.*, ii, 60, p. 692; i, 12, 14.   [23] *Ibid.*, i, 44.   [24] *Ibid.*, i, 7.

[25] *Ibid.*, i, 43.   [26] *Ibid.*, i, 43.   [27] *Ibid.*, i, 27.

[28] *Ibid.*, ii, 18, p. 691.

[29] *Ibid.*, i, 57. *Freedom of the Will*, ch. i, sec. iii. *Cf. Locke.*

[30] *Ibid.*, ii, 59 cor., p. 681.   [31] *Ibid.*, ii, 4, p. 679.

[32] *Ibid.*, ii, 2, p. 678.   [33] *Ibid.*, ii, 11, p. 680.

[34] Edwards' illustration leaves out *continuity* in trying to explain identity. He merely shows that *similarity* does not make identity.

[35] *Notes on Mind*, ii, 72.

[36] In his work on *Original Sin.*

[37] *Notes on Natural Science, Series* ii, No. 48.

CHAPTER V

1. *Edwards' Idealism*

EDWARDS' reputation as a philosopher has been based chiefly on his work on the Will, but he has another and perhaps even greater title to a high place among the world's thinkers in his ideal theory. His exposition of this system is contained in the different collections of *Notes* written before his active life as a minister began, most of them during his life as a college student. We find a statement of his theory in one of his earliest essays, that on *Being*, introductory to the *Notes on Natural Science*. It begins with a discussion of the impossibility of conceiving a state of nothing;[1] to say that thing is not is the aggregate of all contradictions. It is necessary that some being should eternally be. Further it is as great a shock to the mind to think of pure nothing being in one place at any time as it is to think of it in all places or at all times. Hence, he concludes, being must exist everywhere and at all times. "So we see that there must be a necessary eternal being, infinite and omnipresent.' This being can not be solid, for solidity surely is nothing but resistance to other solidities. Space is this necessary eternal infinite and omnipresent being. We find we can with ease conceive how other things should not be. We can remove them out of our minds and place some other in the room of them, but space is the very thing that we can never remove and conceive of its not being. But I had as good speak plain, I have already said as much as that Space is God. . . . And how doth it grate upon the mind to think that something should be from all eternity and yet nothing all the while be conscious of it. To illustrate this, let us suppose the world had a being from all eternity and had many great changes and wonderful revolutions, and all the while nothing knew it, there was no knowledge in the universe of any such thing. How is it possible to bring the mind to imagine this? Yea, it is really impossible it should be that anything should exist and nothing know it. Then you will say, if it be so it is because nothing has any existence but in consciousness. No, certainly nowhere else but either in created or uncreated consciousness. Suppose there were another universe merely of bodies, created at a great distance from this, created in excellent order, harmonious motions and a beautiful variety, and there was no created intelligence in it, nothing but senseless bodies and nothing but God knew anything of it. I demand where else that universe would have a being but only in the divine consciousness. Certainly in no respect. There would be figures and magnitudes and motions and proportions, but where? Where else except in the Almighty's knowledge? . . . Let us suppose for illustration this impossibility, that all spirits in the universe were for a time deprived of their consciousness and that God's consciousness at the same time were to be intermitted. I say the universe, for that time would cease to be of itself, and this not merely, as we speak, because the Almighty could not attend to uphold it, but because God could know nothing of it. . . . We fancy there may be figures and magnitudes, relations and properties, without any one knowing it. But it is our imagination that hurts us. We do not know what figures and properties are. Our imagination makes us fancy that we see shapes and colors and magnitudes, though nobody is there to behold them. But suppose the creation deprived of light . . . then colors would cease to be. The universe would not differ from the void in this respect. At the same time the universe to be altogether deprived of motion, and all its parts to be at perfect rest. Then the universe would not differ from the void in this respect; there would be no more motion in the one than in the other. Then also solidity would cease. All that we mean or can mean by solidity is resistance; resistance to touch, the resistance of some part of space. This is all the knowledge we can get of solidity by our senses, and I am sure all that we can get any other way. . . . But there can be no resistance if there is no motion. One body can not resist another when there is perfect rest among them. But you will say, though there is no actual resistance, yet there is potential resistance, that is such and such parts of space would resist upon occasion. But this is all I would have, that there is no solidity now; not but that God could cause there to be, on occasion. And if there is no solidity there is no extension, for extension is the extendedness of solidity. Then all figure and magnitude and proportion immediately cease. Put then these suppositions together: that is, deprive the universe of light and motion, and the case would stand thus with the universe: there would be neither white nor black, neither blue nor brown, neither bright nor shaded, pellucid nor opaque; no noise nor sound, neither heat nor cold, neither wet nor dry, neither hard nor soft, nor solidity, nor extension, nor figure, nor magnitude, nor proportion, nor body, nor spirit. What then is to become of the universe? Certainly it exists nowhere but in the Divine Mind. . . . A universe without motion can exist nowhere else but in the mind, either infinite or finite.

" It follows from hence that those beings which have knowledge and consciousness are the only proper and real and substantial beings: inasmuch as the being of other things is only by these. From hence we may see the gross mistake of those who think material things the most substantial beings, and spirits more like a shadow: whereas spirits only are properly substance."

Most of the theses here stated—the necessary existence of being, the necessary existence of space, the impossibility of existence without consciousness, the relative nature of color, motion, solidity, resistance, etc., and finally that conscious beings alone really exist—most of these are repeated and expanded in other places in the *Notes*, some of them with modifications. The necessary existence of being is briefly restated and requires no comment.³ Space is discussed more fully.⁴ " Space, as has been already observed, is a necessary being, if it may be called a being : and yet we have also shown that all existence is mental and the existence of all external things is ideal. Therefore it is a necessary being only as it is a necessary idea, so far as it is a simple idea that is necessarily connected with other simple exterior ideas and is as it were their common substance or subject. It is in the same manner a necessary being as anything external is a being." Edwards had changed his point of view since writing his essay on Being. He had there arrived at the conclusion that " space is God," for he had found space to be that which it was impossible to conceive as non-existent ; it was something " necessary, eternal, infinite and omnipresent." He now affirms that space is a necessary idea, something necessarily attaching to all exterior ideas. He did not call it an " *a priori* form " under which ideas of the external world must be received, but it was as necessary to the perception of objects and at the same time as ideal for him as it was for Kant.

He admits that this is not our ordinary conception of space : " for what we call by that name is only colored space and is entirely taken out of the mind if color be taken away : so all that we call extension, motion and figure is gone if color is gone. As to any idea of space, extension, distance or motion that a man born blind might form, it would be nothing like what we call by those names.⁴ And as to the idea of motion that such an one could have, it could be only a diversification of those successions in a certain way by succession as to time."

This leads him to another formulation of the ideal theory, for " as it is very plain color is only in the mind, and nothing

like it can be out of all mind.[5]   Hence it is manifest that there
can be nothing like those things we call by the name of
bodies out of the mind, unless it be in some other mind or
minds."   In short, "that which truly is the substance of all
bodies is the infinitely exact and precise and perfectly stable
idea in God's mind, together with his stable will that the same
shall gradually be communicated to us and to other minds
according to certain fixed and established methods and laws;
or in somewhat different language, the infinitely exact and
precise divine idea, together with an answerable perfectly exact
precise and stable will with respect to correspondent communications to created minds and effects on their minds."

There is still another statement of the argument under the
head of *Existence*.[6]   From the fact that color exists only in
the mind, he argues that nothing in body has any existence
outside the mind.   Color, he holds, has the chief share in our
idea of body.   Color, and figure which is the termination of
color, together with some powers, such as the power of resist-
ing and motion, etc., wholly make up what we call body. . .
If color exists not out of the mind, then nothing belonging to
body exists out of the mind but resistance which is solidity,
and the termination of this resistance with its relations which
is figure, and the communication of this resistance from space
to space which is motion, though the latter are nothing but
modes of the former.   Therefore, there is nothing out of the
mind but resistance, and not that either when nothing is
actually resisted.   Then there is nothing but the power of
resistance.   And as resistance is nothing else but the actual
exertion of God's power, so the power [of resistance] can be
nothing else but the actual exertion. . . . The world is therefore an ideal one."

Again under the head of *Substance*[7] we find still another
proof of his theory.   He argues that the real " being " (essence)
of substance is solidity.   But solidity depends on action.   We
get a notion of solidity only from observing the arrest of mo-

tion at the limits of some parts of space. But to set up or arrest motion or action belongs only to active voluntary beings. There is no reason in the nature of the thing itself why a body when set in motion should stop at such limits more than at another. He concludes that we are right in looking for some substance upholding the properties of bodies, some cause of our ideas, but " that something is He by whom all things consist."

There are other expressions of idealism to be found in Edwards' early writings, but these are the most important and they are sufficient to show that he had clearly conceived the doctrine. It gave him a ready explanation of the connection of mind and body or of mind and brain : " it is nothing but the connection of the operations of the soul with these and those modes of its own ideas or those mental acts of the Deity." He realizes that there is great danger of confusion in this manner of speaking, and we may after all " speak in the old way as properly and truly as ever." [8]

We have noticed that Edwards had much to say about atoms and atomic theories, and that his remarks have been highly estimated by prominent scientists. We shall here only cite one passage wherein he gives a hint of a possible theory of evolution. " It is certain," he says, " that when God first created matter or the various chaoses of atoms, besides creating the atoms and giving the whole chaos its motion, he designed the figure and shape of every atom and likewise their places . . . and this he so ordered that without doing anything more, the chaoses of themselves, according to the established laws of nature, were brought into these various and excellent forms adapted to every one of God's ends." [9] We do not mean to urge that Edwards had worked out any definite theory of evolution, or even conceived of it very clearly, but this passage shows that such a conception would not have been foreign to his thought. It is true that he excepts " plants and animals " from this process, not because he thinks it impossible that they should originate in this way, but because it was " fit and proper that God should have an immediate hand in their creation." For the inorganic world, however, he thinks no such immediate creation necessary.

[1] This is strikingly like Parmenides. Edwards may have known of his doctrines through Cudworth.

[2] Edwards' doctrine of the one substance has more than once been compared to Spinoza's.

[3] *Notes on Mind*, ii, 12, p. 668.   [4] *Ibid.*, ii, 9, 13, pp. 673-4.

[5] Edwards had read Newton.

[6] *Notes on Mind*, ii, 27, 28, 30, 34, 51, 36, 40, pp. 668-673. In this connection he quotes from *Cudworth's Intellectual System* the description of Plato's "Subterranean Cave."

[7] *Notes on Mind*, ii, 61, 25, pp. 674-7.   [8] *Ibid.*, ii, 34, p. 669.

[9] *Notes on Natural Science*, ii, 88. Edwards' interest in the atomic theory may have been aroused by reading Cudworth on the *Greek Atomists*.

CHAPTER VI

JONATHAN EDWARDS (CONTINUED)

1. *Ethical System*

EDWARDS' ethical system may be classed with those which make perfection the end of conduct. In the *Freedom of the Will* there are some implications of hedonism, particularly in his doctrine of motives, where he says that the strongest motive is that which appears most pleasant or agreeable. But this is not the view of the end of action in his principal work on ethics, *The Nature of True Virtue*. The doctrines expressed in that work are supplemented by his treatise on *God's End in the Creation of the World*, and his posthumously published *Lectures on Charity and its Fruits*. Before taking up these we may notice an earlier expression of his views in the *Notes on Mind*. It is found under the essay entitled *Excellency*.[1] His inquiry is like the ethical speculations of the Greeks in that it is a search after " the good," the *summum bonum*. This *summum bonum* Edwards calls " excellency." Excellency, he says, has never been properly defined, though it is that with which we are chiefly concerned. Indeed we are concerned with nothing else. Some have said that excellency is harmony, symmetry or proportion, but that is not a satisfactory definition, for these terms are capable of further explanation. Proportion is an equality or likeness of ratios. Hence excellency would seem to consist in equality. All beauty consists in similarness, in identity of relation. Bodies having similar relations agree. If bodies have no similar relations their lack of them is a deformity, because being disagrees with being, and this lack of agreement must be disagreeable to perceiving being, because whatever disagrees with being must necessarily be disagreeable to being in general, to everything that partakes of entity, and of course to perceiving being. " And what agrees with being must be agreeable to being in general, and therefore to perceiving being; but agreeableness to perceiving being is pleasure, and its contrary is pain. Disagreement or contrariety to being is an approach to nothing which is the greatest and only evil. Entity is the greatest and only good. This is a universal definition of excellency—the consent of being to being, or being's consent to entity. All excellency may be resolved into entity or existence. Being or existence is what is necessarily agreeable to being, and when being perceives it, it will be an agreeable perception ; and any contradiction to being or existence is what being, when it perceives, abhors."

Greatness (quantity of being) is the more excellent not only because it contains a greater capacity for excellence, but is in itself more excellent, as it partakes more of being. If it dissent from being it is the more odious for the same reason. God is the infinite, universal, all-comprehensive existence; as He includes all being in Himself, He cannot be otherwise than excellent. Hence God infinitely loves Himself because His being is infinite.

The agreement of bodies is but a shadow of excellency, as bodies have no proper being of their own. There is no proper consent but that of minds, even of their wills : which when it is of minds towards minds, is love. Wherefore all the primary and original beauty or excellence that is among minds is love.

When we speak of being in general we may be understood to speak of the divine being, for he is an infinite being. As to bodies, we have shown that they have no proper being of their own. And as to spirits, they are the communications of the Great Original Spirit, and doubtless in metaphysical strictness, He is and there is none else.

Virtue, the excellency of spirits, is love of being; God's excellence must be love to himself, as he is the sum of all being.

The divine love reaches all being with perfect purity and sweetness, since all are the communications of himself.

"Happiness consists in the perception of these three things: of the consent of (other) being to its own being; of its own consent to being, and of being's consent to being." "Conscience is the sense the mind has of this consent."

Such in brief is the ethical theory as presented in the *Notes on Mind*. When the *Nature of True Virtue*[2] was written, Edwards had read Hutcheson, Hume, and others, but his doctrine remained essentially the same. The term "virtue" replaces "excellency" in the later work.

Virtue is beauty, but not all beauty is virtue. Virtue is a beauty of perceiving being, having its seat in the mind; it is the beauty of the moral nature, of acts that are attended with desert or worthiness, praise or blame. These acts have their seat in the disposition or will. True virtue renders the exercises of the "heart" truly beautiful; it is the beauty which appears when the act is viewed in all its relations. It must be distinguished from that particular beauty which a thing or act may have within a limited sphere. This latter is not true beauty and hence is not true virtue. "True virtue most essentially consists in benevolence to being in general:[3] it is that consent, propensity and union of heart to being in general that is immediately exercised in a general good-will."

Every intelligent being is related to being in general and is part of the universal system of existence. Its general and true beauty can be nothing but its union and consent with the great whole. If benevolence be directed only to a limited system or a small circle, even if it is not inconsistent with unity to the whole, it is not true virtue, though it may be good in some respects.

It is generally admitted that virtue consists in love,[4] in general benevolence or kind affection. This means that the disposition must be towards benevolence to being in general, not that being in general must be the immediate object of every particular act. Love to particular beings may arise from general benevolence; indeed he who has this disposition will be more disposed than others toward benevolent affection for particular beings, for to these he will have most frequent occasion for exerting his benevolent temper.

Love may be of two kinds; benevolence or love to being, and complacence or love to beauty. Since virtue is the beauty of an intelligent being, and consists in love, complacence, which is love to beauty or virtue can not itself be the primary virtue; for that would make virtue the original ground of itself; virtue can not be both cause and effect. Hence we must find its foundation in something other than itself. Gratitude can not be the primary ground of virtue, for gratitude presupposes benevolence, which is virtue.

We can only conclude that the primary cause of virtue is being simply considered.[5] There may be true virtue in love to beauty or virtue, but being considered in itself is the first object of virtuous love. The second object of virtuous benevolence is benevolent being. Loving a being on this ground necessarily arises from pure benevolence, and comes to the same thing. He that has a good will to general existence must love that temper in others. That being which truly and sincerely seeks the good of others, must approve and love that which joins with him in seeking the good of others. This general benevolence will extend to all being, inclining to the highest general good and to each being whose welfare is consistent with the highest good. Since being simply considered is the first object of benevolence, and since the greater the being is, the greater is its amount of existence, the greater is the benevolence due to it, all other things being equal.

The value of true virtue is in proportion to the degree of existence which the being has, compounded with the degree of his benevolence. True virtue then must chiefly consist in love to God,[6] the Being of beings, infinitely the greatest and best of beings. He has the greatest share of existence, and He is infinitely the most beautiful and excellent. All true virtue must essentially consist in love to God, love both of benevolence and complacence. He is the fountain and foundation of all being and all beauty. We may exercise benevolence toward Him in rejoicing in His happiness and the promotion of His glory, for this is the end for which He created the world.

Love to particular beings, or to a limited circle, if not subordinated to benevolence to being in general, is not of the nature of true virtue, and will pursue the interest of its particular objects in opposition to general existence. Only that love which is subordinated to love to God can be of the nature of true virtue. Hence the virtue of the divine mind must consist in love to himself, and his love to created beings is derived from and subordinate to his love for himself. Virtuous love of created beings to each other will arise from the temper of mind wherein consists a disposition to love God supremely, for all love that is the fruit of true benevolence is virtuous. The best evidence of true virtue in moral beings is their agreement with the end for which God created them, and this end is His own glory.[7]

There are other dispositions, affections of the mind, and principles of action that are often called virtuous. There is a beauty in inanimate objects; such beauty is observable throughout nature not only in these objects, but in living beings and in society. This may be called natural beauty; it consists in uniformity of nature, form, etc.; it is grateful to us by a law of nature or an instinct implanted in us. Such beauty in intelligent beings will be a consequence of benevolence to general being, but cannot be its ground. That it is not true virtue is evident from the fact that men may be gratified by it without recognizing its ground, whereas true or spiritual beauty is pleasing because its ground (union, agreement) is perceived. If this natural beauty were true beauty, the delight which men have in it would be in proportion to their virtue, but this is not the case. Just affections have a beauty superior to the uniformity which there is in them, for they contain an expression of benevolence to universal being. The natural affections as, for example, justice, may agree with the will and command of God, and, in many respects, tend to his glory and the general good.

In order to give a just exposition of Edwards' view, it is necessary to examine his criticism of other doctrines. He considers first the theories which make self-love the motive to virtuous acts.[8] He begins by an examination of the meaning of the term. "Self-love is generally defined as a man's love to his own happiness. This may mean that he loves whatever pleases him, which is the same as to say he loves what he loves, and this proposition admits of no discussion. Self-love commonly means a man's regard to his own private personal interest and pleasures. Love to others may be the effect of self-love. Love to those that love us is no more than a certain expression of self-love, and is not true virtue. The difference between the sentiments which we feel toward animate beings and toward things which are inanimate, arises from the difference in the objects themselves; it does not require any principle other than self-love to explain feelings such as anger and gratitude, which we have toward other persons, but do not have toward inanimate objects. For gratitude, for example, does not necessarily arise from a truly virtuous benevolence, though there is a truly virtuous gratitude. Affections to those bound to us by the ties of nature may be properly referred to self-love as their source. In the same way we may love qualities and characters on account of association, as a child may be pleased by the picture of fruit. In short, a man may from self-love disapprove malice, envy, and other hurtful vices, and on the same principle approve benevolence, charity and the social virtues in general. Undoubtedly some have a love to these virtues from a higher principle, but there is generally in mankind a sort of approbation of them which arises from self-love. There are no particular moral virtues whatever that do not from a sense of desert, association of ideas, and in other ways, come to have some kind of approbation from self-love without the influence of a truly virtuous principle, nor any particular vices that do not by the same means meet with some disapprobation.

Edwards, in this criticism, has maintained that a man might possess all the so called virtues, yet if he is not actuated by a disposition benevolent to being in general, none of his acts would be truly virtuous.

He next considers the moral sense theory.[9] True virtue, he says, does not arise from natural conscience. The disposition a man has to be uneasy in the consciousnes of doing to others what he should be angry with them for doing to him, is a consciousness of being inconsistent with himself, and as it were against himself in his own actions. It may be looked upon as in some way arising from self-love. Self-love implies an inclination to act as one with ourselves, which naturally renders a sensible inconsistence with ourselves in our acts to be a source of uneasiness to the mind. To do to others what we would not have them do to us, is both to choose and refuse, as it were, the same thing. This sort of approval or disapproval is quite different from approving or disapproving actions, because in them we are united to or agree with being in general. The former is a private natural principle, the latter a truly benevolent and divine principle.

The natural conscience arises spontaneously from our putting ourselves in others' places, which is the only way in which we can have any notion of the thoughts, feelings or desires of others. Natural conscience consists (1) in this disposition to approve or disapprove conduct towards others in so far as we are or are not consistent with ourselves, and (2) in the sense of desert, which consists in [a feeling which demands] a natural proportion and harmony between injury and punishment or between kindness and its reward. Approbation and disapprobation of conscience will extend to all virtue and vice in a mind which will take things in general into consideration. For as all virtue or moral good may be resolved into love to others, either God or creatures, so men easily see the uniformity and natural agreement there is between loving others and being accepted and favored by them. This natural conscience, though not tasting the essential beauty of true virtue, may approve of it from that uniformity, equality and justice there is in it. Men by natural conscience may see the justice there is in yielding all to God since they receive all from him, and the justice there is in supreme love to him who gives all well being. Natural conscience if well-informed will approve of true virtue and condemn the want of it. That moral sense which is natural to mankind, so far as it is disinterested and not founded in association of ideas, is the same as this natural conscience. It is admitted that there may be a moral sense, a sense of moral good and evil not founded in self-love, but it is not different from natural conscience, which includes a sense of desert. But this moral sense or natural conscience is not of the nature of a truly virtuous taste arising from a virtuous benevolence. If it were, it would always be in proportion to the virtuous temper of the mind, but this is not true, since a man of vicious temper may have stronger convictions of conscience than one who is virtuous.

There are various dispositions natural to man which are called instincts.[10] They are of many kinds; those which are called social instincts or kind affections may have the appearance of benevolence, and so in some respects resemble virtue, but none of them can be of the nature of true virtue, and would not be if they included all the universe exclusive of God. Pity is one of these natural instincts, and there is a truly virtuous pity, but the natural disposition to it is not truly virtuous; still it has something that belongs to the general nature of virtue, that is love. In many of the natural affections there is love, but it is "private" and short of truly virtuous benevolence in its nature and object. These instincts may have partly the same influence and effect as benevolence. Their defect is that they are confined to a private sphere and do not arise from benevolence to being in general. If that private system contained the sum of universal existence, then their benevolence would have a true beauty. The reason why men are so ready to take them for true virtue is the narrowness of their views, especially their liability to leave the Deity out of account.

These affections have a true negative moral goodness, since their absence is evidence of positive moral evil; they also tend to the good of mankind and to the restraint of evil.

Edwards discusses lastly the theory that sentiment is the basis of virtue.[11] Virtue is a certain kind of beautiful nature, form or quality observed in things. Beauty is immediately perceived and is not arrived at by a process of reasoning. In this sense it is true that virtue is founded in sentiment. But if founded in sentiment means that the inward sense whereby the mind delights in beauty is given arbitrarily, and that the Creator might have given a contrary sense which would have agreed as well with the nature of things, then it is not true. Virtue is cordial consent or union of being to being in general. That frame of mind which is disposed to be pleased with this, is virtuous. To assert that a contrary temper might be virtuous would be to suppose that opposition to being in general might be more agreeable to it than agreement. By the former temper a man agrees with his own being and nature, for he is part of being in general. He must agree with himself for every being that has understanding, and will necessarily loves his own being; if his temper should be inclined to the misery of being in general, then it would be inclined to his own misery, which is inconsistent.

The fact that persons and nations differ as to what is good and evil is used as an argument for the theory that virtue and vice are arbitrary and determined by sentiments; but this argument is not well founded, since the general disposition of the mind may be the same in all, though the objects and occasions differ by reason of example, custom, education and association. Good and evil are not altogether unfixed and arbitrary; they could not be used consistently unless there was uniformity in connecting them with praise or blame.

2. *Doctrine of the Will*

Edwards' greatest work, that on which his reputation as a metaphysician has rested, was the *Inquiry into the Modern Prevailing Notions of the Freedom of the Will.*[12] Although this was written with the avowed purpose of defending his theology against the attacks of opponents, his argument is for the most part purely philosophical. A large part of the work is devoted to the purpose of answering objections to his own view of the question, and to attacking the theories of his opponents. The following is an attempt to present briefly Edwards' own doctrine. He had, as has already been said, accepted the two-faculty psychology of Locke. This imperfect classification of the mental powers was the source of much confusion. To the will was ascribed every mental act that could not be included under the understanding. The will is defined as " that by which the mind chooses; the faculty of the will is the faculty by which the mind is capable of choosine; an act of will is an act of choice." [13] There is some confusion in this definition, but the obvious purpose is to identify will and choice. Choosing includes refusing; preference and desire are not distinct from will or choice. Besides these choosing includes " approving, disapproving, liking, disliking, embracing, rejecting, determining, directing, commanding, forbidding, inclining or being averse, being pleased or displeased with."[14] Inclination is also synonymous with will, which must also include affections, emotions and passions. Choice, moreover, is a comparative act,[15] wherein the mind acts with reference to two or more things that are compared. Thus, according to Edwards, these acts are each and all acts of will.

" Determining the will "[16] is causing that an act of will or

choice should be thus and not otherwise. The determination
of the will supposes an effect which must leave a cause. If the
will be determined, there must be a determiner. . . . That
which determines the will is that motive which, as it stands in
the view of the mind, is the strongest. . . . By motive I
mean the whole of that which moves, excites or invites the
mind to action, whether that be one thing singly or many
things conjointly. Everything that is properly called a motive
has some sort and degree of tendency or advantage to move
or excite the will previous to the effect, or to the act of will.
This previous tendency of the motive is what I call the
strength of the motive. This strength of the motive depends
on the nature and circumstances of the thing viewed, the
nature and circumstances of the mind that views, and the degree and manner of its view."

"But it is, perhaps, unnecessary to mention the state or the
nature and circumstances of the mind, as it is a determining
factor in the other two elements and is included in them.
Whatever influences the mind is viewed as a good . . . and
the will is always as the greatest apparent good . . . To appear good to the mind is the same as to appear agreeable or
seem pleasing to the mind. The act of will always follows the
last dictate of the understanding in this sense, that "the soul
always wills or chooses that which in the present view of the
mind, considered in the whole of that view and all that belongs
to it, appears most agreeable." It is difficult to understand just
what Edwards means to make of deliberation. This last expression would seem to place it among the acts of the understanding, but he has made the "comparative act" as well as
the resulting decision, an act of choice or will. The distinction of motive from will is also far from clear. The "state of
the mind" was, as it seemed, the deciding element in determining the strength of the motive. If by this state of the mind
he means perception or judgment, then the understanding
determines the strength of the motive, and hence the will. If

he means by this term such states as being pleased or displeased with the object presented, then, since these are acts of will, the will determines itself, and this he considers an absurdity. His whole analysis is so imperfect and so confused as to make his subsequent arguments anything but conclusive.

His third section is concerned with the explication of terms. Necessity, as he proposes to use it, is "philosophical necessity," which is nothing else than the full and fixed connection between the things signified by the subject and predicate of a proposition. Necessity may be natural or moral. Moral necessity as here used indicates the necessity of connection and consequence arising from such moral causes as strength of motives or inclinations, and their connection with certain volitions and actions. Natural necessity is, for him, physical necessity. Moral necessity differs from it not in the nature of the connection, but rather in the nature of the terms connected *i. e.*, the causes and effects connected are "moral," not physical.

Necessity in the ordinary sense implies voluntary opposition. Such opposition is impossible in moral necessity, which is a certainty of the inclination of the will itself. Moral inability consists in the opposition or want of inclination to perform a certain act. Contingency as here used means that an event comes to pass without an adequate cause. Freedom in common speech means the power, opportunity or advantage that any one has to do as he pleases.[17] In this sense it can be ascribed only to what has will, and consequently not to the will itself. But liberty as used by some writers consists in a self-determining power in the will, whereby it is independent in its determinations on any cause without itself. This conception of liberty includes also indifference, *i. e.*, that the mind previous to the act of volition is in equilibrium; it includes also contingence. A moral agent is a being capable of action, that can, in a moral sense, be denominated good or evil. A moral agent possesses a moral faculty, a capacity of being influenced in his actions by moral inducements or motives.

In order to show Edwards' own attitude it will be well to look for a moment at his arguments against the opposite view. His opponents supported, as he believed, a doctrine of the will which included self-determination, "indifference" and contingence. By self-determination he understood them to mean that the will itself determined all its free acts, or that the soul in the exercise of a power of willing is the determiner. If the soul can determine its acts it can only do so by choosing them, for the will doubtless governs its own free acts as it does those of the body, that is, by antecedent volitions. Then the will determines a free act by an antecedent choice, and this again by one preceding it, and so on *ad infinitum* unless we come to an act wherein the will is not self-determined, and hence not free in this notion of freedom. If to evade this it be said that the will does not determine its own acts of choice by a preceding act of choice, but only that the soul in the use of the faculty or power of will determines its own volitions, and that it does this without any act going before the act determined; such an evasion would be grossly absurd. First, if the soul in the exercise of that power determines it, that is the same thing as for the soul to determine volition by an act of will, for the exercise of the power of will is the same as an act of that power. Secondly, if a power of will determines the act of will, then the power of choosing determines it; but if a power of choosing determines the act, it does it by choosing it; here again we have an act of will determined by a preceding act of choice. Thirdly, to say that the soul determines its own volition, but not by an act, is a contradiction; for directing, deciding or determining is an act. If the will determines itself it must be active in so doing, for the will can determine nothing if it be not active in determining, and if the will is active in determining a volition then the determination is an act of will. If it be said that the will is not active in determining, then it exercises no liberty. If any should say that the determining act is not before the determined act, but that the exertion of the act is the determination of the act, it would still remain to answer what influence directs or determines the mind to such a conclusion or choice as it does. If the will does this, it must do so by a preceding act.[18] To say that the will or mind orders, influences and determines itself to exert an act by the very exertion itself, is to make the exertion both cause and effect.

Edwards' argument against contingence is the argument that an effect cannot take place without a cause. By cause he here means "any antecedent, natural or moral, positive or negative, on which any event depends, in whole or in part, for its existence or manner of existence, whether the antecedent have any positive efficiency or not." It includes not only efficient causes, but also occasions. His argument against "indifference" is that it is self-contradictory, for it supposes that the mind wills and is at the same time indifferent. If it is indifferent, how does it exercise choice? If it is indifferent before the choice is made, but not indifferent in making the choice, then the choice is not free. He affirms that even if the will were the cause of the acts, the acts would be determined, and hence necessary and not free effects.

These are his main arguments against the self-determining power of the will. Their weak points are obvious, and it is not necessary to consider them here. His confused use of the terms will and motive, and his unwarrantable extension of the meaning of cause, which he uses as if it were always *causa efficiens*, are fatal weaknesses. His greatest difficulty was to make his doctrine of will consistent with moral agency. He makes the will the proper object of command. "The first and determining act is properly the subject (object) of command; it is in this act that obedience or disobedience lies especially." Virtue and vice lie in these acts, for "the essence of virtue and vice of dispositions lies not in their causes, but in their nature." If the vice of a vicious act lay not in itself, but in its cause, then the vice of this cause would lie not in itself, but in its cause, and so on *ad infinitum*. Hence if the virtue or vice is anywhere, it is in the nature of the act itself. But Edwards does not explain why it lies in the act of the will rather than in any other act in the series of causes and effects.

He endeavors to prove that moral necessity is compatible with responsibility by an appeal to common sense. His argument is that men commonly hold that a man is responsible for his action if he does as he pleases in performing the action. He does not prove, however, that men do not commonly ascribe to a free intelligent being the power of alternate choice, and until this is proved his appeal to common sense is not valid.

Edwards asserts repeatedly that he believes that men are free, but by freedom he means only absence of restraint and constraint. He does not admit what is now called freedom of spontaneity, but asserts that even if this were granted it would not prove the self-determining power of the will. It would still remain to determine why such an act was performed and not some other. It is self-determination, the power of alternate choice, that he attacks. Besides the arguments already cited, he makes use of the theology accepted by both himself and his immediate opponents, but these arguments do not require notice here. He repels the objection that his doctrine makes men no more than mere machines. " I would say that man is entirely, perfectly and unspeakably different from a mere machine, in that he has reason and understanding with a faculty of will, and so is capable of volition and choice." He does not show us, however, that his doctrine of " understanding, will, volition and choice " does not make machines of these very acts and faculties.

CONCLUSION

After the time of the men we have considered there was a long period in which activity in philosophy was very much limited. Edwards' work on the Will called forth many works in its criticism and in its defence. One of the latest and best was the able criticism of Rowland G. Hazard, *Freedom of the Mind in Willing*, New York, 1864. Many others would be worthy of mention in a more extensive discussion of American thought.

With the exception of the *Freedom of the Will*, few of these early writings have received much attention. Political questions began to absorb all the attention of the people. With the establishment of an independent government the energy of the people was more than ever directed to the development of material resources. Idealism did not meet with general favor, and the doctrines based upon it were neglected. The Common Sense Philosophy which came to be so widely accepted did not stimulate original thinking. Philosophy was kept within the limits of Theology ; but, as in the Medieval Period, the schools of Theology alone offered opportunities for the study of Philosophy ; but again, as in the Medieval Period, the increasing independence of the two subjects promises to be of advantage to both.

[1] *Notes on Mind*, ii, 1, 14, 62, 63, 64, 39, 45, pp. 693–702.

[2] *Works* (ed. Dwight), vol. iii, pp. 93–157.   [3] *Ibid.*, p. 94.

[4] *Cf. Charity and its Fruits*, especially lecture viii.

[5] Vol. iii, p. 97.   [6] Chap. ii.

[7] This is the doctrine of his work on *God's End in Creation*.

[8] Vol. iii, Ch. iv.   [9] *Ibid.*, Ch. v.   [10] *Ibid.*, Ch. vi.

[11] *Ibid.*, Ch. viii.   [12] *Works*, vol. ii, pp. 15–300.

[13] *Ibid.*, p. 15.   [14] *Ibid.*, pp. 16–18.   [15] *Ibid.*, p. 92.

[16] *Ibid.*, part i, sec. ii.   [17] *Ibid.*, part i, sec. v.

[18] His opponents could ask how a motive could determine an act without a preceding act.

BIBLIOGRAPHY

AMERICAN PHILOSOPHY

Bancroft, Geo. *History of United States*, vols. ii, iii, iv.
Burt, B. C. *History of Modern Philosophy.*
Błakey, Robt. *History of Philosophy of Mind.*
Carlson, J. C. *Om Filosofien i Amerika*, Upsala, 1895.
Fisher, G. P. *Discussions in History and Theology*, 227–252.
Lyon, Georges. *L'Idealisme en Angleterre*, ch. ix, x.
Maurice, F. D. *Moral and Metaphysical Philosophy.*
McCosh, Jas. *Scottish Philosophy*, ch. xxiii.
Sanborn, F. B. *Journal Speculative Philosophy*, xvii, 401.
Smyth, E. C. *Proceedings of American Antiquarian Society*, Oct., 1895, 1896.
Uhden, H. F. *The New England Theocracy.*
Ueberweg, Fr. *History of Philosophy.*
Falkenberg. *History of Philosophy.*
Frothingham. *Transcendentalism in New England.*
Bibliotheca Sacra, 42 : 496. G. Campbell.
     47 : 1. N. E. Wood.
British Quarterly, 25 : 88.
Catholic World, 42: 91. R. M. Johnston.
Church Quarterly, 26 : 124.
Educational Review, 10 : 1. A. C. Armstrong, Jr.
Educational Review, 13 : 10. A. C. Armstrong, Jr.
Mind, 4: 89. G. S. Hall.
Nation, 31 : 93. T. Davidson.
Westminster Review, 33: 345.

JONATHAN EDWARDS

Allen, A. V. G. *Life of Edwards.*
Chalmers, Thos. *Christian and Civic Economy*, i, 318–322.
Dexter, F. B. *Yale Biographies and Annals.*
Dwight, S. E. *Memoir of Edwards.*
Fisher, G. P. *Discussions in History and Theology*, 227–252.
    History of the Christian Church, ch. viii.
Fraser, A. C. *Notes to Works of Locke and of Berkeley*, passim.
Godwin. *Political Justice*, i, 301.
Hall, Robert. *Works.*
Hazard, R. G. *Freedom of the Mind in Willing.*
Histories of Yale and Princeton Colleges.
Holmes, O. W. *International Review*, July, 1880.
Hopkins, Samuel. *Life of Edwards.*
Huxley, T. H. *Art. Edwards, Encyclopedia Brittanica.*
Lyon, Georges. *L'Idealisme en Angleterre*, ch. x.
Mackintosh. *Progress of Ethical Philosophy.*

Miller, Samuel. *Life of Edwards.*
Porter, Noah. *Historical Discourse on Bp. Berkeley*, 1885.
Rogers, H. *Introduction to Bohn's Edition of Edwards' Works.*
Stephen, Leslie. *Hours in a Library*, ii, 41–106.
　　　　　　　English Philosophy in the Eighteenth Century.
Taylor, Isaac. *Introduction to Edition of Edwards on the Will.*
Trumbell. *History of Connecticut.*
Tyler, M. C. *History of American Literature.*
Uhden, H. F. *The New England Theocracy.*
In addition to the above, v. *Bibliography of American Philosophy* and a mass of periodical literature, easily found by reference to an index.

EDWARDS' WORKS

Worcester, 1808–9, 8 vols, 8vo.
London, 1817, 8 vols, 8vo, vols. ix and x added, Edinburgh, 1847.
London, 1834, 2 vols.
London, 1809, 8 vols.
New York, 1829–30, 10 vols, 8vo.　S. E. Dwight's edition.
New York, 1844, 2 vols, vols. iii and iv added.　New York, 1846.
New York, 1855.　Worcester edition reprinted.
London, 1847, 10 vols, 8vo.
Lectures on Charity and its Fruits, New York, 1852.
Freedom of the Will.
Boston, 1754, 8vo.
London, 1762.
London, 1768.
Wilmington, 1790.
Among the works occasioned by the *Freedom of the Will,* may be mentioned those of Jos. Smalley, Jon. Edwards, Jr., Stephen West, Samuel West, Jas. Dana, A. T. Bledsoe, Fred'k Beasley, D. D. Whedon, R. G. Hazard, H. P. Tappan, Jer. Day, N. W. Taylor.

SAMUEL JOHNSON.

Beardsley, E. E. *Life and Correspondence of Samuel Johnson.*
Chandler, T. B. *Life of Samuel Johnson.*
Lyon, Georges. *L' idealisme en Angleterre*, ch. ix.
Autobiography (unpublished).
Histories of Yale and Columbia Colleges.
American Journal of Education, 27 : 449.
A few other unimportant articles in periodicals.
For Works, see sketch of Life.

WILLIAM BRATTLE

Quincy, Josiah. *History of Harvard University.*
Massachusetts Historical Society Collections, 2d Series, vol. vii, 55–6.